Great Designs for
Shaped Beads

Tilas • Peanuts • Daggers

Anna Elizabeth Draeger

KALMBACH BOOKS

Kalmbach Books
21027 Crossroads Circle
Waukesha, Wisconsin 53186
www.Kalmbach.com/Books

Some of the projects in this book have appeared previously in *Tiles & Tilas* (ISBN 978-0-87116-496-4), *Peanuts & Berries* (ISBN 978-0-87116-497-1), and *Daggers & Drops* (ISBN 978-0-87116-498-8).

ISBN: 978-0-87116-495-7

E ISBN: 978-0-87116-758-3

Editor: Mary Wohlgemuth
Art director: Lisa Bergman
Technical editor: Jane Danley Cruz
Layout artist: Rebecca Markstein
Illustrator: Kellie Jaeger
Photographers: James Forbes, William Zuback

Library of Congress Cataloging-in-Publication Data
Draeger, Anna Elizabeth.

   Great designs for shaped beads : tilas, peanuts, daggers / Anna Elizabeth Draeger.

      p. : col. ill. ; cm.

   ISBN: 978-0-87116-495-7

   1. Beadwork–Handbooks, manuals, etc. 2. Beadwork–Patterns. 3. Jewelry making. I. Title. II. Title: Shaped beads

TT860 .D73 2012
745.594/2

CONTENTS

INTRODUCTION

So many new bead shapes are on the market—tile shapes…peanut beads…drops and daggers… Do you see these cool and unusual shapes and wonder how to use them? Sometimes shapes that are out of the ordinary can pose difficulties when trying to incorporate them into your beadwork, but they also provide wonderful design opportunities. This book includes ideas for using each type of bead shape and, in the last section, you'll find projects that combine several shapes in a single jewelry piece. The projects also call for a supporting cast of beads such as Japanese seed beads and Swarovski Elements crystals and pearls.

With the help of the illustrations that accompany each project, most beaders—even motivated beginners—shouldn't have trouble stitching any of them. The projects incorporate my favorite stitches, including peyote stitch, herringbone, right-angle weave, netting, and a few other beadweaving techniques. If you need a quick lesson on any of the techniques used, such as adding and ending thread, jump to p. 84.

I used Fireline 6-lb. test as beading thread for all the projects and #12 beading needles, keeping a few slimmer #13s nearby in case I had any trouble fitting the needle through the beads (some of the designs require several thread passes). You can use your favorite thread and larger or smaller needles as needed. Use even, moderately tight tension as you work. I suggest holding the beadwork in your hands instead of placing it on a work surface. When you work a stitch, pinch the thread where it exits the last bead, and don't let go until you've completed the next stitch. This can take some practice but is worth the effort, resulting in a polished, professional-looking piece of jewelry.

Another way to achieve a professional result is to use quality findings that either match your beadwork or act as a focal piece where appropriate. These days, that doesn't necessarily mean they are made of precious metal; many of the findings I used in these projects are base metal, but they are well-designed, high-quality components that harmonize with my designs.

. . . .

This book contains projects that appeared in the digital editions *Tiles & Tilas*, *Peanuts & Berries*, and *Daggers & Drops*, as well as nine all-new projects.

Miyuki Tila bead

Czech two-hole tile bead

Tiles & Tilas

For this project book, I created six designs that showcase the unique characteristics of Miyuki Tila beads and Czech two-hole tile beads. Both beads are flat, square, glass beads with two holes. Tila beads have fairly sharp corners compared with the Czech version. Czech two-hole tile beads have rounded edges and are thicker than Tila beads. Either style will work for most of the designs, but where one works better, only that style is listed in the supplies needed for that project.

Currently, Tila beads are available in 60 colors including translucent and opaque beads, with metallic, matte, AB, and satin finishes (which have a fabulous sheen). Czech tile beads are available in 100 colors, many with unusual finishes. (You'll sometimes find Czech tile beads with just one hole rather than two—be sure yours have two for these projects.) Both styles are beautiful and inspiring, and manufacturers are developing more options all the time.

Peanuts & berries

Peanut beads—which you may see called farfalle, bowtie, dogbone, butterfly, bubble, or double-bubble beads—have soared in popularity as beaders discover more ways of stitching with them.

Peanut beads are distributed by Czech and Japanese manufacturers. You'll find Czech beads on strands or hanks and Japanese beads in tubes or bags. Standard peanut beads are approximately 2x4mm. The Japanese manufacturer Miyuki makes a similar shape called Berry beads, and these beads are slightly thicker (about 2.5x4.3mm). Although you shouldn't mix bead types within a project, most projects can be made with any peanut-style bead.

You can see some of the subtle differences between the manufacturers' versions of the peanut shape in the photos on the right.

You'll discover many different colors and special finishes for peanut beads. Some options are opaque, metallic, matte, matte metallic, color-lined, permanent finish, and hybrid colors—a range that provides a wide, delightful color palette.

You may notice discrepancies among the peanut bead shapes. If the glass around the hole of the bead is very thin, it could break as you make several thread paths through it, so it is best to discard these. Berry beads don't have this issue because the glass is thicker near the hole.

Peanut beads

Berry beads

Czech peanuts

Peanut shapes strung together

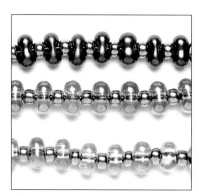

With seed beads as spacers

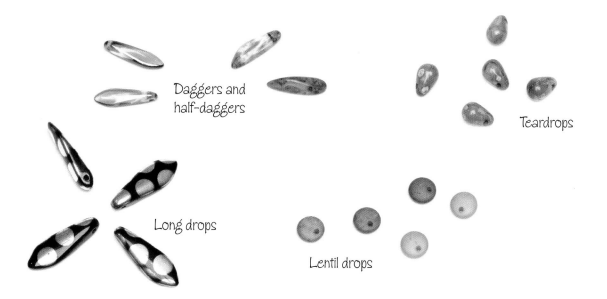

Daggers and half-daggers

Teardrops

Long drops

Lentil drops

Daggers & drops

Daggers and drop beads come in a huge variety of shapes and sizes. I used several styles in the projects, including dagger beads of different sizes, teardrops, magatama fringe beads and long drops, and some unusual shapes like lentil drops and petal-shaped drops.

Many daggers and drops are pressed glass of Czech origin. Dagger beads come in several sizes and styles. The most common dagger sizes are 3x10mm–7x17mm, and they

are sold in many colors and finishes, often on hanks. You may see half-daggers, which are rounded on one edge and flat on the other, and a 5x16mm two-hole style of dagger. Pressed-glass drops, often referred to as petals, come in a large range of sizes. Other shapes including teardrops, pear-shaped, duck-bill drops, and leaves are all drilled across the top so they hang like a drop bead.

Some of the drops are considered seed beads. Magatama drop beads (sometimes called fringe beads) and long drops can

be irregular in shape, so it is best to inspect the beads to find the ones that are most similar. It isn't necessary to discard odd-shaped drops, but grouping similar drops together will provide the most even stitches. This is most evident with the long drops, and you can sort these beads easily by stringing several on your needle all facing the same direction. Any beads that seem out of the ordinary can be set aside for another project.

Happy stitching!

Each project includes a design option or two to give you ideas for stitching a variation on the main project. As you work, you may discover even more ways to incorporate the techniques or components into your own designs.

I hope you enjoy beading these projects!

Anna

Tila Diamonds

Tila beads set on edge with right-angle weave create a central diamond motif. Stack several rows for a bracelet that drapes beautifully around your wrist.

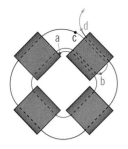

fig. 1

fig. 2
Top view

fig. 3
Bottom view

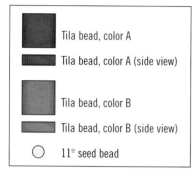

■	Tila bead, color A
▬	Tila bead, color A (side view)
■	Tila bead, color B
▬	Tila bead, color B (side view)
○	11º seed bead

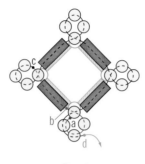

fig. 4
Bottom view

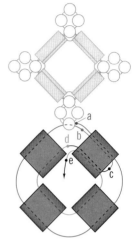

fig. 5

SUPPLIES
Bracelet, 7 in. (18cm)
- 96 Tila beads, color A
- 44 Tila beads, color B
- 5–6 grams 11º seed beads
- 3-strand clasp
- 6 4–6mm jump rings
- Fireline 6-lb. test
- Beading needles, #12
- 2 pairs of chainnose pliers

COLORS
Matte black bracelet
Tila beads: Miyuki TL401, matte black (color A); Miyuki TL2002, matte metallic silver-gray (color B)
11º seed beads: Miyuki 4222, Duracoat galvanized pewter

Matte/shiny bronze bracelet
Tila beads: Miyuki TL2006, matte metallic bronze (color A); Miyuki TL457, metallic bronze (color B)
11º seed beads: Toho Y302, hybrid jet picasso

Green/ivory bracelet
Tila beads: Miyuki TL2008, matte metallic bronze (color A); Miyuki TL2592, satin ivory (color B)
11º seed beads: Toho 547, gold- lustered green tea

1 On 2 yd. of Fireline, pick up four color-B Tila beads, leaving a 12-in. tail. Sew through the same hole of the first B again **[fig. 1, a–b]**.

2 Sew through the remaining hole of the same B your thread is exiting in the opposite direction **[b–c]**. Continue sewing through all the remaining holes of the next three Bs in the ring, and the same hole of the first B your thread exited in this step to form a loose diamond shape **[c–d]**. The four holes you just sewed through will be considered the top holes of the diamond.

3 Pick up an 11º, and sew through the next B. Repeat this step three times to add an 11º between each top hole of the Bs **[fig. 2]**, and then sew through the other hole of the same B your thread is exiting in the opposite direction.

4 Pick up an 11º, and sew through the next B. Repeat this step three times to add an 11º between each bottom hole of the Bs **[fig. 3]**. Exit an 11º.

5 Pick up three 11ºs, and sew through the 11º your thread exited at the start of this step **[fig. 4, a–b]**. Sew through the bottom hole of the next B and 11º **[b–c]**. Repeat this step three times to add a picot to each 11º on the bottom of the diamond shape. Exit a center 11º of one of the picots **[c–d]**.

6 Pick up four Bs, and sew through the 11º your thread exited at the start of this step **[fig. 5, a–b]**. Sew through the bottom hole of the first B again **[b–c]**. Sew through the remaining hole of the same B your thread is exiting in the opposite direction **[c–d]**. Sew through all the top holes of all four Bs in the ring to form the next loose diamond shape **[d–e]**.

7

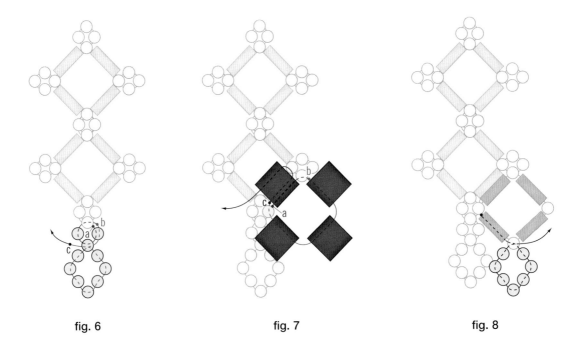

<table>
<tr><td align="center">fig. 6</td><td align="center">fig. 7</td><td align="center">fig. 8</td></tr>
</table>

tip **As you add each diamond shape, make sure you position the top holes of the As and Bs on the same side of the picots.**

7 Repeat steps 3–6, but in step 4, pick up only 11°s between three of the bottom holes of the Bs, and skip the 11° connecting the new diamond to the previous picot. In step 5, you will add only three picots instead of four. Each time you complete a diamond, sew through the bottom beads to exit the center 11°s of the picot opposite the join.

8 Repeat steps 6 and 7 nine times, or until you reach the desired length minus 1 in. (2.5cm). This will be the center row of the bracelet.

9 At the end of the center row, pick up three 11°s, and sew back through the 11° your thread exited at the start of the step **[fig. 6, a–b]**. Repeat to add a third picot on this end **[b–c]**.

You may want to pick up seven 11°s for the end picot instead of three if your jump rings are thick; you will attach the clasp to this end picot. I picked up seven to accommodate my jump rings.

Retrace the thread path of the last three picots, and end the working thread. Using the tail, repeat this step on the other end of the center row.

10 Add a new length of thread on one end of the strip, leaving a 12-in. (30cm) tail, and exit the side 11° of the picot next to the end diamond from the center row **[fig. 7, point a]**. Make sure your thread points toward the other end of the bracelet.

11 Pick up a color-A Tila bead, and sew through the bottom 11° in the next side picot from center row **[a–b]**. Pick up three As, and sew through the 11° your thread exited at the start of this step **[b–c]**.

12 Work the thread through the top and bottom holes of the As to form a loose diamond shape as before. Work steps 3 and 4, but in step 4, pick up only an 11° for the remaining two bottom holes. Skip the existing 11°s from the picots in the center row when sewing through the bottom four holes of the As. The bottom 11° along the edge of the side row of As will not have picots added.

13 Using the tail, sew through the next A and the following 11°. Pick up the same number of beads you picked up for the third picot added in step 7 **[fig. 8]**. Reinforce the beads added in this step, and end the tail.

14 Using the working thread, sew through the beadwork to exit the top 11° of the next side picot from the center row **[fig. 9, point a]**. Pick up an A, and sew through the side 11° of the next connecting picot from the center row **[a–b]**. Pick up an A, and sew

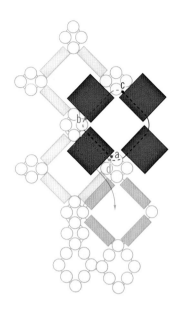

fig. 9

through the bottom 11º of the next side picot from the center row [b–c]. Pick up two As, and sew through the 11º your thread exited at the start of this step [c–d] and the next A. Sew through the remaining hole of the same A your thread is exiting. Work the thread path through the top holes to form a loose diamond, and then work steps 3 and 4, but in step 4, pick up only an 11º for the remaining bottom hole. Skip the existing 11ºs from the picots in the center row when sewing through the bottom four holes of the As. The bottom 11º along the edge of the side row of As will not have a picot added. Repeat this step until you reach the other end, and then work one unit as in steps 12 and 13, adding the picot to the other end of the row. End the working thread.

15 Work a third row of As off the other side of the center row as in steps 10–14. Attach a clasp to the end picots with jump rings.

design options bracelets

Use Czech two-hole tile beads to make a chunkier version of this bracelet. Substitute size 8º seed beads in place of the 11ºs. Or, make a single strand for a delicate alternative.

COLORS

Matte/shiny black/gray bracelet
Two-hole tile beads in place of Tila beads: Czech, jet (color A); Czech, matte iris purple (color B)
8º seed beads in place of 11º seed beads: Toho 989, bronze-lined crystal

Single-strand braclet
Tila beads: Miyuki TL1865, opaque smoke grey luster
11º seed beads: Toho 401, opaque black

Triangulation

String tile beads and 10º cylinder beads to create a comfortable base for peek-a-boo pearls or a little crystal glimmer. Stack tiles en pointe for an unusual profile.

SUPPLIES

Bracelet, 6 in. (15cm)
- 45 Czech tile beads
- 15 3mm bicone crystals or pearls
- 3–4 grams 10º round or hex cylinder beads, or 1.5mm cube beads
- 1–2 grams 11º cylinder beads
- 1 gram 15º seed beads
- Clasp
- 2 4mm jump rings
- Fireline, 6-lb. test
- Beading needles, #12
- 2 pairs of chainnose pliers

COLORS

Black bracelet
Tila beads: Miyuki TL401F, matte opaque black
3mm bicone crystals: Swarovski, garnet satin
10º hex-cut cylinder beads: Miyuki 0021, steel metallic
11º hex-cut cylinder beads: Miyuki 0021, steel metallic
15º seed beads: nickel-plated

Olive green bracelet
Tila beads: Miyuki TL2008, matte metallic patina iris
3mm pearls: Swarovski, light green
1.5mm cube beads: Toho F458, matte metallic khaki iris
11º cylinder beads: Toho 617, matte dark olive
15º seed beads: Toho 457, gold-lustered green tea

Green/bronze bracelet
Czech tile beads: Persian turquoise, Picasso finish
3mm bicone crystals: Swarovski, sand opal
10º cylinder beads: Miyuki 0254, bronze luster
11º cylinder beads: Miyuki 0254, bronze luster
15º seed beads: Toho 995, dichroic-lined aqua AB

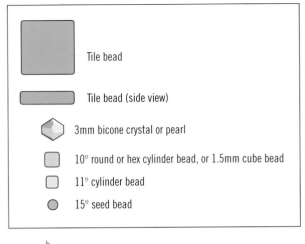

Tile bead

Tile bead (side view)

3mm bicone crystal or pearl

10º round or hex cylinder bead, or 1.5mm cube bead

11º cylinder bead

15º seed bead

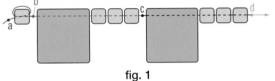

fig. 1

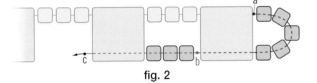

fig. 2

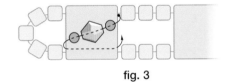

fig. 3

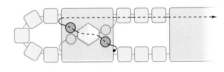

fig. 4

1 On 2 yd. (1.8m) of Fireline, attach a stop bead, leaving a 12-in. (30cm) tail [fig. 1, a–b]. Sew through one hole of a tile bead and pick up three 10º cylinder beads [b–c]. Repeat the pattern [c–d] until you reach the desired length, minus the length of your clasp. End with a tile bead.

2 Pick up five 10ºs, and sew through the remaining hole of the end tile bead [fig. 2, a–b]. Pick up three 10ºs, and sew through the remaining hole of the next tile bead [b–c]. Repeat until you reach the first tile bead on the other end. Pick up five 10ºs, and sew through the other hole of the end tile bead to make a loop for the clasp.

3 Pick up a 15º seed bead, a 3mm bicone crystal or pearl, and a 15º. Sew through the other hole of the same tile bead so the beads just added lie diagonally across the tile bead [fig. 3].

4 Pick up a 15º, sew through the 3mm, and pick up a 15º. Sew through the other hole of the same tile bead, the next three 10ºs, and the corresponding hole of the next tile bead [fig. 4].

5 Repeat steps 3 and 4 for the length of the bracelet. End the working thread and tail.

6 Add 2 yd. (1.8m) of Fireline to one end of the bracelet, and exit a center 10º before the first base tile bead on one side of the bracelet [fig. 5, point a]. Pick up an 11º cylinder bead, one hole of a tile bead, an 11º, a 15º, an 11º, one hole of a tile bead, and an 11º, and sew through the center 10º before the next base tile bead [a–b]. Repeat this stitch along this side of the bracelet, exiting the second 10º in the clasp loop [fig. 6, point a].

7 Pick up a 15º, and sew through the end 10º [a–b]. Pick up a 15º, and sew through the next 10º [b–c].

8 Pick up an 11º, and sew through the remaining hole in the last tile bead picked up in step 6. Pick up an 11º, a 15º, and an 11º, and sew through the remaining hole of the next tile bead picked up in step 6. Pick up an 11º, and sew through the

center 10º before the next base tile bead. Repeat along this side of the bracelet, then repeat step 7 on the other end.

9 Retrace the thread path along the first side of the bracelet, skipping the 15ºs to pull the peaks into a tight angle.

tip **You may have to poke the tip of your needle through the 15º as you pull the working thread so the 15º pops up, forming the point.**

10 Sew through the end beads, and then repeat step 9 on the other side of the bracelet. End the working thread.

11 Open a jump ring, and attach half of the clasp to one end of the bracelet. Repeat on the other end of the bracelet.

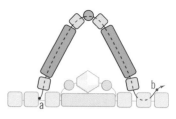

fig. 5

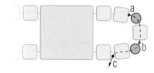

fig. 6

design option ring

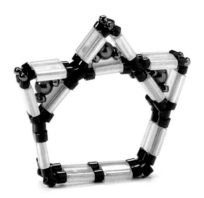

On 2 yd. (1.8m) of Fireline, pick up a pattern as in step 1 for a total of seven tile beads and seven sets of 10ºs. Tie the beads into a ring, exiting a tile bead. Sew through the other hole of the same tile bead to change direction, add three 10ºs between each tile bead, and exit a tile bead. Embellish the next three tile beads as in steps 3 and 4 of the bracelet. Sew through the beadwork to exit a center 10º on one side of the ring in the set of 10ºs before the next embellished tile bead. Work as in steps 6 and 8 to add three peaks over the 3mms. Retrace the thread path, and end the thread.

tip **To adjust the band size, omit some of the 10º cylinders at the base of the ring. For my size-8 ring, I used only one cylinder per Tila bead hole at the base, and as I reinforced the thread path around the ring, I skipped the center cylinders at the lower corners to snug up the size.**

Marvelous Mosaics

Stack Tila beads back-to-back to align the pairs of holes. Stitch them together to make a mini mosaic design for your wrist!

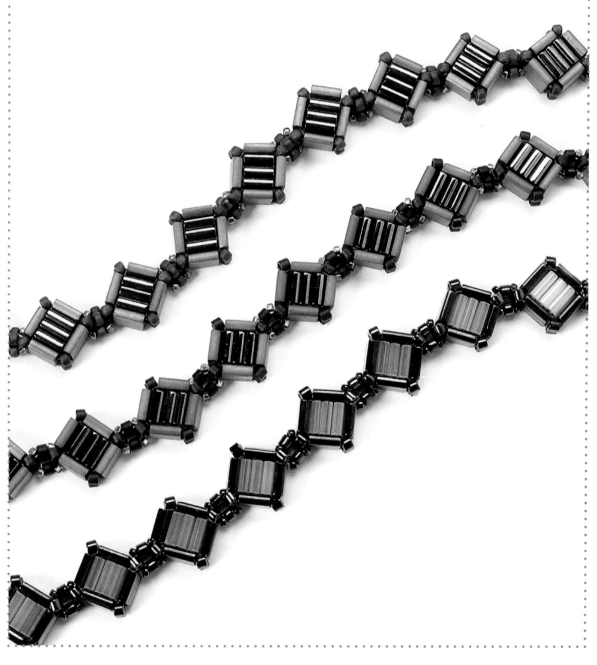

SUPPLIES

Bracelet, 6¼ in. (15.9cm)
- 44 Tila beads, color A
- 33 Tila beads, color B
- 2–3 grams 10º cylinder beads
- 1–2 grams 15º seed beads
- Clasp
- 2 4mm jump rings
- Fireline, 6-lb. test
- Beading needles, #12
- 2 pairs of chainnose pliers

COLORS

Black bracelet

Tila beads: Miyuki TL2002, metallic gray AB (color A); Miyuki TL464, hematite (color B)

10º cylinder beads: Miyuki 0310, matte black

15º seed beads: Miyuki 464A, nickel plated

Green bracelet

Tila beads: Miyuki TL2008, matte metallic green iris (color A); and Miyuki TL468, metallic green iris (color B)

10º cylinder beads: Miyuki 0327, matte metallic teal iris

15º seed beads: Miyuki 650, moss green silver-lined AB

Brown bracelet

Tila beads: Miyuki TL458, brown metallic iris (color A); and Miyuki TL2592, cream satin (color B)

10º cylinder beads: Miyuki 0007, brown metallic iris

15º seed beads: Miyuki 458, brown iris

▬	Tila bead (side view), color A
▬	Tila bead (side view), color B
▪	10º cylinder bead
●	15º seed bead

fig. 1

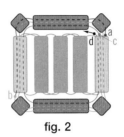

fig. 2

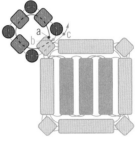

fig. 3

1 On 1 yd. (.9m) of Fireline, sew through one hole of a color-A Tila bead and one hole of a color-B Tila bead, leaving a 10-in. (25cm) tail. Sew through the same hole of the A, stacking the two Tila beads next to each other. Retrace the thread path, and exit the B **[fig. 1, a–b]**. The thread path will be connecting the bottom holes of the Tila beads.

2 Sew through the bottom hole of a new B, and sew through the bottom hole of the previous B. Retrace the thread path, and exit the new B. Repeat this step for a total of three stacked Bs **[b–c]**.

3 Sew through the bottom hole of a new A, and sew through the bottom hole of the previous B. Retrace the thread path, and exit the new A **[c–d]**.

4 Sew through the top hole of the A your thread exited at the start of this step, and work a thread path through the top holes of the stack of the Tila beads to mimic the thread path through the bottom holes. Exit the top hole of the end A.

5 Pick up a 10º cylinder bead, and sew through the top hole of a new A. Pick up a 10º, and sew through the top hole of the A on the opposite end of the stack **[fig. 2, a–b]**. Repeat this step **[b–c]**, and retrace the thread path through the top holes of the As surrounding the Bs, skipping the 10ºs to pull the As into a tight square shape. Exit an A **[c–d]**.

6 Sew through the bottom hole of the A your thread exited at the start of this step, pick up a 10º, and sew through the bottom hole of the next A. Repeat around to add a 10º to each bottom corner. Retrace the thread path, skipping the 10ºs. End the working thread.

7 Using the tail, exit a bottom 10º, then pick up three 10ºs. Sew back through the bottom 10º your thread exited at the start of this stitch, and retrace the thread path through the 10ºs **[fig. 3, a–b]**. Exiting one of the bottom 10ºs, pick up a 15º seed bead, and sew through the next bottom 10º in the ring. Repeat around **[b–c]**, retrace the thread path, and end the tail.

8 Repeat steps 1–6.

9 Using the tail, exit a bottom 10º, and pick up a 10º. Sew through a bottom 10º in the previous unit opposite the ring of beads created in step 7. Pick up a 10º, and sew through the bottom 10º your thread exited at the start of this stitch **[fig. 4]**. Retrace the thread path of the four 10ºs, pick up a 15º, and sew through the next bottom 10º in the ring. Repeat around, retrace the thread path, and end the tail.

10 Make a total of 11 units (or as many units needed to achieve the desired length), connecting each unit to the previous one, opposite the connecting ring. For the last unit, don't end the working thread, but make a ring of beads as in step 7 on the remaining end.

11 Attach half the clasp to one end of the bracelet with a jump ring. Repeat to attach the other half of the clasp to the remaining end of the bracelet.

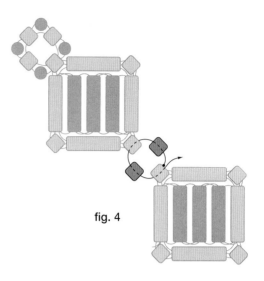

fig. 4

design option earrings

COLORS
Tila beads: Miyuki TL2005, matte
    metallic dark raspberry iris
    (color A); Miyuki TL301, dark
    topaz rainbow gold luster (color B)
10º cylinder beads: Miyuki 680,
    matte metallic green/pink
15º seed beads: Toho 703, matte
    cabernet

1 Make two units as in steps 1–6 of the bracelet.

2 Using the tails, make rings of beads as in step 7 off the bottom 10º and the top 10º on the same corner of each unit.

3 Hang the drops from a hoop-style earring, or run a jump ring through both rings of beads and attach the drop to an earring finding.

15

St. Pete Meets Tila

St. Petersburg chain produces a feminine, feathery band of beadwork. Stitch Tila beads and crystals into a fashionable bracelet.

SUPPLIES

Bracelet, 6½ in. (16.5cm)
- About 26 Tila beads
- 52 4mm bicone crystals
- 2 grams 15º seed beads
- 1 gram 11º seed beads
- Clasp
- 2 4mm jump rings
- Fireline, 6- or 8-lb. test
- Beading needles, #12
- 2 pairs of chainnose pliers

COLORS

Gold bracelet

Tila beads: Miyuki TL462, gold iris

4mm crystals: Swarovski, white opal AB 2X

11º seed beads: Miyuki 3101, rose gold luster

15º seed beads: Miyuki 462, metallic gold iris

Purple bracelet

Tila beads: Miyuki TL401FR, black opaque matte AB

4mm crystals: Swarovski, cyclamen opal

11º seed beads: Miyuki 9312, lilac gold luster

15º seed beads: Miyuki 2212, lined aqua AB

tip It's important to retrace the thread path while repeating steps 4–6 or the bracelet will twist between the Tila beads and will not lie flat.

1 On 2 yd. (1.8m) of Fireline, attach a stop bead, leaving a 10-in. (25cm) tail. Sew through the right hole of a Tila bead and the left hole of a second Tila bead [fig. 1].

2 Pick up an 11º seed bead, a 4mm bicone crystal, and three 15º seed beads. Skip the three 15ºs, and sew back through the 4mm, the 11º, the left hole of the last Tila bead added, and the right hole of the previous Tila bead [fig. 2, a–b]. Pick up five 15ºs, and sew through the left hole of the same Tila bead [b–c].

3 Pick up an 11º, a 4mm, and three 15ºs. Skip the three 15ºs, and sew back through the 4mm, the 11º, and the left hole of the Tila bead [fig. 3, a–b], the first two 15ºs (skipping the center 15º), and the last two 15ºs in the end loop [b–c]. Sew through the right hole of the Tila bead, the left hole of the next Tila bead, and all

the beads in the fringe, exiting the 11º at the top of the fringe [c–d]. Using gentle tension, sew through the right hole of the last Tila bead [d–e], centering the fringe under the hole it exits. This keeps the path clear for the next Tila bead that will be added.

4 Pick up an 11º, a 4mm, and three 15ºs. Skip the three 15ºs, and sew back through the 4mm, the 11º, and the right hole of the Tila bead your thread exited at the start of this step [fig. 4, a–b].

5 Sew through the left hole of a new Tila bead, and pick up an 11º, a 4mm, and three 15ºs. Skip the three 15ºs, and sew back through the 4mm, the 11º, and the same hole of the last Tila bead [b–c].

6 Reinforce the last two steps: Continue through the right hole of the previous Tila bead and the beads in the fringe above it. Sew down through the right hole of the same Tila bead, the left hole of the last Tila bead added, the beads in the fringe below it, and, using gentle tension, the right hole of the last Tila bead added.

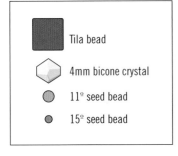

	Tila bead
	4mm bicone crystal
	11º seed bead
	15º seed bead

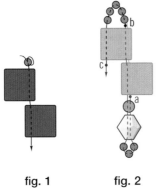

fig. 1   fig. 2

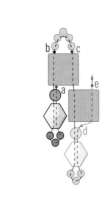

fig. 3

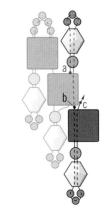

fig. 4

7 Repeat steps 4–6 until you reach your desired length minus the length of the clasp, and then repeat step 4.

8 Sew through the left hole of a new Tila bead, pick up five 15ºs, and sew through the right hole of the same Tila bead. Pick up an 11º, a 4mm, and three 15ºs. Skip the three 15ºs, and sew back through the 4mm, the 11º, and the same hole of the last Tila bead. Sew through two 15ºs, skip a 15º, and sew through the next two 15ºs and the left hole of the Tila bead **[fig. 5]**. Retrace the thread path through the last few fringe and Tila beads, and end the working thread, remove the stop bead, and end the tail.

9 Attach a clasp to each end of the bracelet with jump rings.

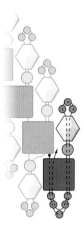

fig. 5

. . . .

design option necklace

COLORS
Tila beads: Miyuki TL462, gold iris
4mm crystals: Swarovski, purple velvet
11º seed beads: Miyuki 336, dark rose yellow-lined
15º seed beads: Miyuki 462, metallic gold iris

To make a necklace, simply attach a chain to each end of the bracelet, and attach half of the clasp to each end of the chain.

Zigzag Trellis

Stringing different quantities or sizes of beads between opposite holes of Tila beads produces a zigzag effect. Make a dainty bracelet or necklace with a single row, or explore the options for linking two or more rows for a lacy latticework band.

SUPPLIES

Single-row bracelet, 7³⁄₈ in. (19cm)

- 24 Tila beads
- 1–2 grams 15º seed beads
- 1–2 grams 11º seed beads
- Fireline, 6-lb. test
- Beading needles, #12 or #13
- Clasp or multistrand clasp
- Quantity of 4mm jump rings equal to number of loops of the clasp
- 2 pairs of chainnose pliers

COLORS

Tila beads: Miyuki TL421B, opaque cream pearl

3mm bicone crystals: Swarovski, olivine

11º seed beads: Miyuki 460H, gold-bronze metallic iris

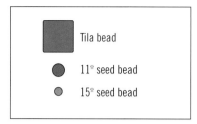

- ⬛ Tila bead
- 🔴 11º seed bead
- 🔵 15º seed bead

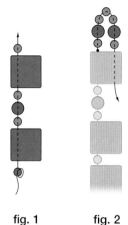

fig. 1   fig. 2

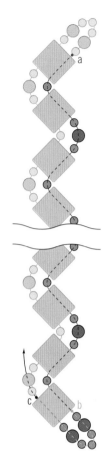

fig. 3

tip Bead quantities above are for a single-row bracelet. Multiply by the desired number of rows if you're making a multi-row version (see p. 21).

First row

1 On 2 yd. (1.8m) of Fireline, attach a stop bead, leaving a 10-in. (25cm) tail.

2 Sew through one hole of a Tila bead, and pick up a 15º seed bead, an 11º seed bead, and a 15º. Sew through one hole of a Tila bead and pick up a 15º [fig. 1]. Repeat this pattern until you have 24 Tila beads, or until you're a little past your desired length. (If you're making more than one row, be sure to end with an even number of Tila beads.) The row will shorten a bit as you add a second row of seed beads to the remaining holes of the Tila beads.

3 To make a loop at the end of the row, pick up a 15º, an 11º, three 15ºs, an 11º, and a 15º, and sew through the remaining hole of the end Tila bead [fig. 2].

4 If you have a single bead between the last two Tila beads, pick up a 15º, an 11º, and a 15º, and sew through the remaining hole of the next Tila bead. If you have three beads between the last two Tila beads, pick up a 15º, and sew through the remaining hole of the next Tila bead. Continue down the length of the bracelet, adding a 15º, an 11º, and a 15º next to the single bead, and a 15º next to the set of three beads, sewing through the remaining hole of the next Tila bead each time [fig. 3, a–b].

5 When you reach the other end, check the length, keeping the clasp in mind. Stop here for a bracelet that is a single zigzag row. If you are making only a single row, end with the loops pointing in opposite directions. Make a loop on this end as in step 3 [b–c]. Retrace the thread path, and end the threads. Attach a clasp to the end loops with jump rings.

tip If you are adding subsequent rows, end with the loops pointing in the same direction as shown. If you are making only one row, end with the loops pointing in the opposite direction so the clasp will lie straight.

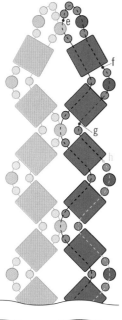

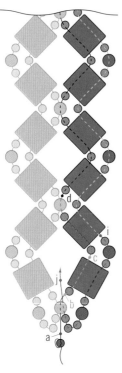

fig. 4

Second row

1 On 2 yd. (1.8m) of Fireline, attach a stop bead, leaving a 6-in tail. Sew through the side 11º of the loop on one end of the previous zigzag row [fig. 4, a–b].

2 Pick up a 15º, and sew through one hole of a new Tila bead [b–c]. Pick up a 15º, sew through one hole of a new Tila bead, pick up a 15º, and sew through the next 11º from the previous zigzag row [c–d]. Repeat this step until you reach the last 11º in the previous zigzag row [d–e].

3 Pick up three 15ºs, an 11º, and a 15º, and sew through the remaining hole of the end Tila bead [e–f].

4 Pick up a 15º, an 11º, and a 15º, and sew through the remaining hole of the next Tila bead [f–g].

5 Pick up a 15º, and sew through the remaining hole of the next Tila bead [g–h].

6 Repeat steps 4 and 5 until you reach the second-to-last Tila bead on the other end of the bracelet [h–i]. Repeat step 4 to exit the last Tila bead. Finish the end loop by picking up a 15º, an 11º, and three 15ºs, and sewing through the side 11º next to the stop bead [i–j]. Retrace the thread path, and end the threads.

For each additional pair of rows, work steps 1–5 as described for the first zigzag row. Work steps 1–6 as for the second row, but in steps 4 and 6, sew through an 11º along one edge of a previous pair of rows to join the two pairs together.

7 Use jump rings to attach a multistrand clasp.

design options earrings, rings, and multi-row bracelets

The instructions on the previous page show you how to turn a single zigzag into a multi-row bracelet by mirroring the position of the rows.

Make a pair of zigzag earrings by working a short single row.

To make a ring, pick up an even number of repeats to fit around your finger (the band will shrink as you work the second thread path of the first row), and tie the beads into a ring. Add a seed bead edging to a single row, or make two rows to produce a wider band.

COLORS

Earrings
Tila beads: Miyuki TL301, dark topaz rainbow gold luster
11º seed beads: Miyuki 359, light topaz-lined aqua
3mm crystals: Swarovski, olivine

Single-row ring
Tila beads: Miyuki TL1865, opaque smoke gray luster
3mm bicone crystals: Swarovski, black diamond
2mm round crystals: Swarovski, jet
15º seed beads: Miyuki 401, black

Double-row ring
Tila beads: Miyuki TL3173, transparent oyster luster
11º seed beads: Dyna-mites 4577, silver-lined light gray rainbow
15º seed beads: Miyuki 456, gunmetal iris

Double-row bracelet
Tila beads: Miyuki TL2006, metallic gold matte
11º seed beads: Miyuki 2022, dark creme matte
15º cylinder beads: Miyuki 0031, 24k gold plated

Double-row bracelet #2
Tila beads: Miyuki TL464, hematite
11º seed beads: Toho 9190, nickel plated
15º seed beads: Miyuki 401, black

Four-row bracelet
Tila beads: Miyuki TL401FR, opaque black matte AB
11º seed beads: Toho PF-553, galvanized pink lilac
15º seed beads: Miyuki 0505, higher metallic dragonfly

Six-row bracelet
Tila beads: Miyuki TL468, green gold metallic
10º cylinder beads: Miyuki 0373, matte metallic sage green luster
11º cylinder beads: Miyuki 1053, matte metallic plum emerald gold

Cubic Cuties

Right-angle weave provides the structure for these precise beaded beads. Suspend them as links between chunky lengths of chain, snuggle them in a bracelet, or suspend a pair for earrings.

SUPPLIES

For one bead, ½ x ⁵⁄₁₆ in. (1.3cm x 8mm)
- 4 Tila beads
- 12 2mm round crystals
- 8 3mm bicones
- 1 gram 11º seed beads
- 1 gram 15º seed beads
- Fireline, 6-lb. test
- Beading needles, #12

ADDITIONAL SUPPLIES

Necklace, 28 in. (71cm)
- 14 3mm bicone crystals
- 16 in. (41cm) chain
- 14 in. (36cm) 20-gauge wire
- 2 4mm jump rings
- Clasp (optional)
- 2 pairs of chainnose pliers
- Roundnose pliers
- Wire cutters

Bracelet, 7 in. (18cm)
- 7 6mm crystal rondelles
- 14 4mm bicones
- 1 gram 15º seed beads
- 2 crimp beads
- Clasp
- Beading wire, .014–.015
- Crimping pliers
- Wire cutters

Earrings
- 4 4mm bicone crystals
- 2 headpins
- Pair of earring wires
- 2 pairs of chainnose pliers
- Roundnose pliers

COLORS

Bracelet

Tila beads: Miyuki TL2008
2mm round crystals: Swarovski, crystal silver shade
8mm rondelles: Swarovski, purple haze
4mm bicones: Swarovski, metallic green
3mm bicones: Swarovski, erinite
11º seed beads: Miyuki 361, yellow-lined aqua
15º seed beads: Toho F463B, matte metallic teal iris

Necklace

Tila beads: Miyuki TL206, matte bronze metallic iris
3mm bicones: Swarovski, olivine
3mm bicones: Swarovski, crystal dorado 2X
2mm round crystals: Swarovski, jet
11º seed beads: metallic green iris
15º seed beads: Toho 506, higher metallic june bug

Earrings

Tila beads: Miyuki TL401FR, matte black AB
4mm bicone crystals: Swarovski, purple velvet
3mm bicone crystals: Swarovski, violet opal
2mm round crystals: Swarovski, crystal silver shade
11º seed beads: Toho 384, grape color-lined purple
15º seed beads: Toho F463S, steel blue

For each beaded bead

1 On 1 yd. (.9m) of Fireline, pick up four 3mm bicone crystals. Sew back through the first 3mm to form a ring. Retrace the thread path, exiting the first 3mm picked up [fig. 1, a–b].

2 Pick up an 11º seed bead, and sew through the next 3mm in the ring. Repeat around the ring, and exit through an 11º [b–c].

3 Make four spokes that will create the sides of the beaded bead: Pick up an 11º, and sew through one hole of a Tila bead. Pick up three 11ºs, and sew through the other hole of the same Tila bead. Pick up an 11º, and sew through the 11º your thread exited at the start of this step [fig. 2, a–b]. Sew through the next 3mm and following 11º in the ring [b–c]. Repeat this step three times [c–d].

4 Sew through the next 11º, the adjacent hole of the Tila bead, and the first two 11ºs of the first spoke [d–e]. Pick up a 3mm, and sew through the next center 11º of the three 11ºs of the next spoke [e–f]. Repeat three times, retrace the thread path through the ring of 3mms, and sew through an adjacent 11º.

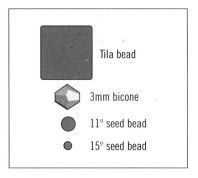

Tila bead

3mm bicone

11º seed bead

15º seed bead

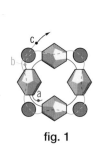

fig. 1

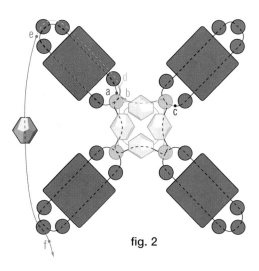

fig. 2

fig. 3

fig. 4

5 Pick up five 15° seed beads, and sew through the next 11° in the ring. Repeat the last stitch three times. Retrace the thread path, skipping the center 15° of each corner stitch to pull the 15°s into a square shape [fig. 3]. Sew through the beadwork to add the corner 15°s to the other end of the beaded bead. Sew through the first two 15°s of the next corner stitch.

6 To embellish the edge, pick up two 15°s, three 2mm round crystals, and two 15°s. Sew through the center 15° at the opposite end of the bead, and back through the last seven beads picked up. Skip the center 15° of the corner stitch, and sew through the next two 15°s, the 11°, and two 15°s of the next corner stitch [fig. 4]. Repeat this step three times, then sew through the beadwork to exit two 15°s of a corner stitch on the opposite end of the beaded bead. Retrace the thread path through the edge embellishments. End the thread.

Bracelet

1 Make six beaded beads.

2 Cut 12 in. (30cm) of beading wire. On one end, pick up a crimp bead and half of a clasp. Go back through the crimp bead and crimp it. Trim the tail.

3 String a 15°. String a pattern of a 4mm bicone crystal, a 15°, an 8mm rondelle, a 15°, a 4mm, and a beaded bead five times, and pick up a 4mm, a 15°, an 8mm, a 15°, a 4mm, and a 15°.

4 Attach the other half of the clasp as in step 2.

Necklace

1 Make seven beaded beads (mine are of assorted colors).

2 Cut six 2-in. (5cm) lengths of chain.

3 Cut 2 in. (5cm) of 20-gauge wire. Make a plain loop on one end of the wire. String a 3mm bicone and a beaded bead, and make another plain loop. Repeat for the remaining beaded beads.

4 Open a loop on one end of the beaded bead, and attach the end link of one of the 2-in. lengths of chain. Open the loop on the other end of the beaded bead and attach a second chain. Repeat with the remaining beaded beads and chains, ending with a beaded bead on each end.

5 Determine the desired finished length, and cut the remaining chain to this length. Open a loop of one of the end beaded beads, and attach it to an end link of the chain. Repeat with the remaining end beaded bead. If desired, cut the center link or links of the chain and attach a clasp to the end links with jump rings.

Earrings

1 Make two beaded beads.

2 On a 1½-in. (3.8cm) headpin, string a 4mm bicone crystal, a beaded bead, and a 4mm. Make a plain or wrapped loop above the 4mm.

3 Open the loop on an earring finding, and attach the loop of the dangle.

4 Repeat to make a second earring.

tip To use Czech tile beads in this project, you need to bump up the seed bead sizes, resulting in a larger beaded bead. Use 8°s in place of 11°s, 11°s in place of 15°s, and 4mm bicone crystals in place of 3mms. The 2mms remain the same.

Berry Baubles

Embellish right-angle weave to make
fun and funky beaded beads. Show off
each one among crystals and pearls in
a necklace, or make more and string
them closely for a bold bracelet.

SUPPLIES

Necklace, 17½ in. (44.5cm)

- 120 Berry beads
- 5–6 grams 11º seed beads
- 4–5 grams 15º seed beads
- 22 5mm bicone crystals
- 12 6mm pearls
- 6 8mm pearls
- 2 crimp beads
- Clasp
- Beading wire, .014
- Fireline, 6-lb. test
- Beading needles, #12
- Crimping pliers
- Wire cutters

COLORS

Berry beads: Miyuki F463K,
   green-pink matte metallic iris

11º seed beads: Miyuki F463K,
   green-pink matte metallic iris

15º seed beads: Toho 460A,
   raspberry bronze iris

5mm bicone crystals: Swarovski,
   golden shadow

6mm pearls: Swarovski,
   dark green

8mm pearls: Swarovski,
   bright gold

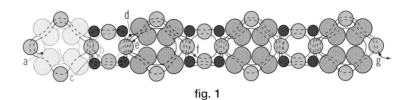

fig. 1

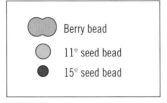 Berry bead	
11º seed bead	
15º seed bead	

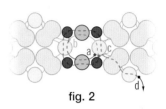

fig. 2

1 On 2 yd. (1.8m) of Fireline, pick up four Berry beads, and sew through the first Berry bead picked up to form a ring, leaving a 6-in. (15cm) tail.

2 Pick up an 11º and sew through the next Berry bead in the ring. Repeat this step three times, and sew through the next 11º, Berry bead, 11º, Berry bead, and 11º [fig. 1, a–b].

3 Pick up three 11ºs, and sew through the 11º your thread exited at the start of this step [b–c]. Pick up a 15º, and sew through the next 11º picked up in this step. Repeat the last stitch three times, and sew through the next 15º, 11º, and 15º, and exit the 11º opposite the 11º connecting the seed bead unit to the Berry bead unit [c–d].

4 Form the next Berry bead unit: Pick up four Berry beads, and sew through the 11º your thread exited at the start of this step [d–e]. Sew through the next Berry bead. Pick up an 11º, and sew through the next Berry bead. Repeat the last stitch twice, and then sew through the next five beads and exit the 11º opposite the 11º connecting the previous 11º unit to the new Berry bead unit [e–f].

5 Repeat steps 3 and 4 twice [f–g].

6 Join the units into a ring: Pick up an 11º, and sew through the end 11º from the first stitch [fig. 2, a–b]. Pick up an 11º, and sew through the end 11º from the last stitch [b–c]. Pick up a 15º, and sew through the next 11º in the connecting ring. Repeat the last stitch three times, and then sew through the nearest Berry bead unit to exit an open 11º along one edge [c–d].

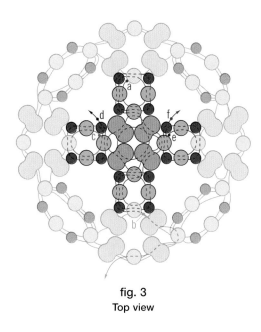

fig. 3
Top view

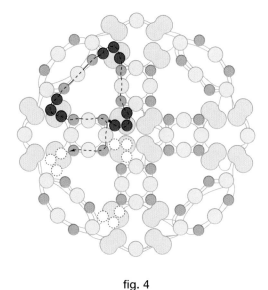

fig. 4

7 Repeat steps 3 and 4, and then work as in step 6 to join the Berry bead unit just completed to the open 11º in the Berry bead unit opposite the 11º your thread exited at the start of this step **[fig. 3, a–b]**. Sew through the next Berry bead, 11º, and Berry bead, and exit the 11º opposite the last join. Repeat this step, but sew through the nearest Berry bead unit to exit an open 11º **[point c]**.

8 Work as in step 6 to connect the remaining open 11ºs between any two adjacent Berry bead units **[c–d]**. Repeat **[e–f]** to connect the remaining Berry bead units.

9 Sew through the 15º, 11º, and 15º on one side of a 11º unit. Pick up three 15ºs, and sew through the 15º, 11º, and 15º from an adjacent 11º unit. Repeat the last stitch twice to create three picots between the 11º units connecting the adjacent Berry bead units **[fig. 4]**. Repeat on all the 11º units, and end the threads. Make a total of five beaded beads.

10 On 24 in. (61cm) of beading wire, string a crimp bead and half the clasp. Go back through the crimp bead, and crimp it. Trim the tail.

11 String seven 11ºs, a 5mm bicone crystal, an 11º, a 6mm pearl, an 11º, an 8mm pearl, an 11º, a 6mm, an 11º, a 5mm, seven 11ºs, a 5mm, a Berry bauble, and a 5mm. Repeat this stringing sequence four more times, and then string seven 11ºs, a 5mm bicone crystal, an 11º, a 6mm pearl, an 11º, an 8mm pearl, an 11º, a 6mm, an 11º, a 5mm, and seven 11ºs.

12 String a crimp bead and the other half of the clasp, and crimp the crimp bead. Trim the tail.

design option ring

Make a single Berry bauble and display it using an interchangeable ring finding. You could also make a pair of these fun beaded beads and string them on a headpin between two crystals to make earrings.

COLORS:
Berry beads: Miyuki BB263, sea foam-lined crystal AB
11º seed beads: Miyuki 4216, Duracoat dark sea foam
15º seed beads: Toho 39, silver-lined tanzanite

Playful Components

Peanut beads nestle together so nicely. Using a combination of peyote stitch and netting techniques produces cute little components that work well in all sorts of accessories.

SUPPLIES

Bracelet, 6¾ in. (17.1cm)

- 8 4mm pearls
- Peanut beads:
  96 color A
  144 color B
- 3–4 grams 15º seed beads
- Clasp
- 2 4–6mm jump rings
- Fireline 6-lb. test
- Beading needles, #12
- 2 pairs of chainnose pliers

COLORS

4mm pearls: Swarovski, burgundy
Peanut beads: 464, nickel plated
 (color A); 457N, burgundy bronze
 (color B)
15º seed beads: Miyuki 464,
 nickel plated .

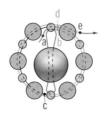

fig. 1

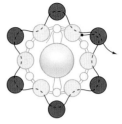

fig. 2

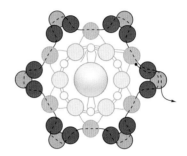

fig. 3

1 On 18 in. (46cm) of Fireline, pick up a 15º seed bead, a 4mm pearl, and a 15º, leaving a 6-in. (15cm) tail. Sew back through the pearl and the first 15º so the working thread and tail exit opposite ends of the 15º [fig. 1, a–b].

2 Pick up a pattern of a color-A peanut bead and a 15º twice, and then pick up an A. Sew through the 15º on the opposite end of the 4mm [b–c]. Repeat [c–d], and then retrace the thread path of the outer ring, exiting an A [d–e]. End the 6-in. tail.

3 Pick up a color-B peanut bead, and sew through the next A in the ring. Repeat five times to complete the round, exiting the first B picked up in this step [fig. 2].

4 Pick up a B, an A, and a B, and sew through the next B in the previous round. Repeat five times to complete the round, retrace the thread path of this round, and exit a center A added in this round [fig. 3].

5 Pick up 11 15ºs, and sew through the A your thread exited at the start of this step. Retrace the thread path, skipping every third 15º to pull the ring into a diamond shape [fig. 4]. End the thread.

6 Repeat steps 1–4 to make another component, then connect it to the previous component: Pick up five 15ºs, and sew through an A on the previous component opposite the ring of 15ºs. Pick up five 15ºs, and sew through the A your thread exited at the start of this step. Retrace the thread path, skipping the center 15ºs [fig. 5]. End the thread.

7 Work as in step 6 for the desired number of components, but for the last component, after completing the join, sew through the outer edge of the beadwork to make a ring of 15ºs as in step 5 opposite the last join. End the thread.

8 Open a jump ring, and attach half of the clasp to an end loop of 15ºs. Repeat on the other end.

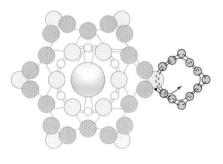

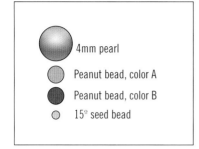

⬤	4mm pearl
◯	Peanut bead, color A
⬤	Peanut bead, color B
◯	15º seed bead

fig. 4

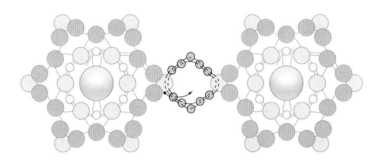

fig. 5

· ·

design option ring and earrings

COLORS

Ring
3mm pearl: Swarovski, cream
Peanut beads: Miyuki 2002,
    metallic olive (color A); Miyuki
    2002MA, metallic olive matte
    (color B)
15º seed beads: Toho 457,
    gold-lustered green tea

Earrings
4mm pearl: Swarovski, burgundy
Berry beads: Miyuki 2441,
    cinnamon gold luster
15º seed beads: Toho 457,
    gold-lustered green tea

To make a ring, repeat steps 1–4 to make one component, but substitute a 3mm pearl instead of a 4mm pearl if desired. Work in a way similar to step 5 to make a band of 15ºs until you reach the desired band size. Connect the band to the opposite A in the component.

Use Berry beads in only one color for the earrings, and work steps 1–3 to make a smaller component. Make a loop as in step 5, and attach an earring finding to the loop.

Peyote Zigzag

The shape of peanut beads adds dimension and weight to beadwork, lending a high-quality look and feel to simple stitches. For this choker, use diagonal peyote stitch to create a sophisticated piece of jewelry with tiny crystals along the edge for just the right touch of sparkle.

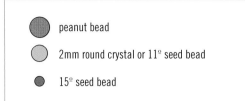
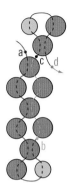

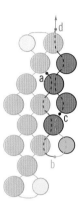

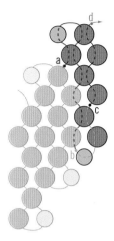

fig. 1   fig. 2   fig. 3

SUPPLIES
Choker, 14¾ in. (37.5cm)
- 25–30 grams peanut beads
- 231 2mm round crystals
  (or 11º seed beads)
- 1 gram 15º seed beads
- 2 4–6mm jump rings
- Clasp
- Fireline 6-lb. test
- Beading needles, #12
- 2 pairs of chainnose pliers

COLORS
Peanut beads: Czech, jet picasso
2mm round crystals: Swarovski,
    crystal silver shade
15º seed beads: black

tip **If you don't like to work with doubled thread, you can use 8-lb. Fireline in place of the doubled 6-lb. Ending and adding thread can be tricky with doubled thread, but if it is too difficult to thread both tails onto one needle to tie them off, simply work with one tail at a time.**

1 On a comfortable length of doubled Fireline, pick up six peanut beads and a 2mm round crystal, leaving a 10-in. (25cm) tail. Skip the 2mm and the last peanut bead picked up, and sew through the next peanut bead toward the tail [fig. 1, a–b].

2 Continue in flat peyote by picking up a peanut bead, skipping a peanut bead from step 1, and sewing through the next peanut bead. Repeat this step [b–c].

3 Work an increase turn: Pick up a peanut bead, a 2mm, and a peanut bead. Slide all three beads up to the bead your thread exited at the start of this step. Skip the last peanut bead and 2mm, and sew back through the first peanut bead added in this step [c–d].

4 Work two stitches using peanut beads [fig. 2, a–b].

5 Work a decrease turn: Pick up a 2mm, and sew back through the last peanut bead added in the previous row [b–c].

6 Work two stitches using peanut beads [c–d].

7 Repeat steps 3 and 4 [fig. 3, a–b].

8 Change direction to form a zigzag: Pick up a 2mm and a peanut bead, and sew back through the last peanut bead added in the previous row [b–c]. Work two stitches using peanut beads [c–d].

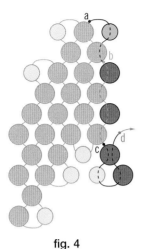

fig. 4

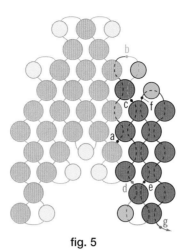

fig. 5

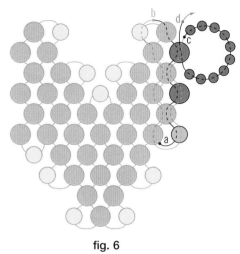

fig. 6

9 Work a decrease turn: Pick up a 2mm, and sew back through the last peanut bead added in the previous row [fig. 4, a–b]. Work two stitches using peanut beads [b–c], and then work an increase turn [c–d].

10 Work two stitches using peanut beads [fig. 5, a–b]. Work a decrease turn [b–c], two stitches with peanut beads [c–d], and then work an increase turn [d–e]. Work two stitches with peanut beads [e–f], and then change direction by picking up a 2mm and a peanut bead, and

sewing through the last peanut bead added in the previous row. Work two stitches using peanut beads [f–g].

11 Repeat steps 9 and 10 until you reach the desired length, ending and adding thread as needed, but in the last repeat of step 10, only work three rows, stopping short of changing direction.

12 To end the last row, work a decrease turn and two stitches using peanut beads [fig. 6, a–b]. Retrace the last two

rows to exit the last peanut bead picked up in the last row [b–c].

13 Pick up 10 15º seed beads, and sew through the peanut bead your thread exited at the start of this step [c–d]. Retrace the thread path several times, and end the thread.

14 Open a jump ring, and attach half of the clasp to an end loop of 15ºs.

15 Repeat steps 12–14 on the other end of the choker.

design option bracelet

You can change the number of peanut beads picked up in step 1 to make a thicker or thinner band. To make this bracelet, I picked up eight peanut beads, and in step 10, I worked two more rows before changing direction to create a thicker band with wider points.

Perennial Path

I love to mix stitches to create unexpected pairings in my jewelry designs. For this bracelet, I started with the easy flow of chevron stitch, added right-angle weave accents, and then worked a second thread path to incorporate peyote stitch.

SUPPLIES

Purple and green bracelet,
8 in. (20cm)
- 112 Berry beads
- 10 grams 11º seed beads

Purple and blue bracelet,
7¾ in. (19.7cm)
- 112 Berry beads
- 5 grams 11º cylinder beads
- 10 grams 11º seed beads

For both bracelets
- Clasp
- 2 4–6mm jump rings
- Fireline 6-lb. test
- Beading needles, #12
- 2 pairs of chainnose pliers

COLORS

Purple and green bracelet
Berry beads: Miyuki 1531,
   sparkling purple-lined
11º seed beads: Toho 338B,
   olivine color-lined emerald

Purple and blue bracelet
Berry beads: Miyuki 2440,
   transparent gray rainbow luster
Aiko cylinder beads: Toho 505,
   blue iris higher metallic
11º seed beads: 39, silver-lined
   purple

Purple and green bracelet

1 On 2 yd. (1.8m) of Fireline, pick up four Berry beads, leaving a 12-in. (30cm) tail. Sew back through the first Berry bead again to form a ring [fig. 1, a–b], and then retrace the thread path several times to hold the ring in place.

2 Pick up five 11º seed beads and four Berry beads. Sew through the first Berry bead just picked up again to form a ring [b–c]. Retrace the thread path of the Berry beads again if you have trouble keeping the beads snug, but make sure to exit the first Berry bead picked up in this step.

3 Pick up seven 11ºs and four Berry beads. Sew through the first Berry bead just picked up again to form a ring [c–d], retracing the thread path if necessary.

4 Pick up five 11ºs, and sew through the Berry bead opposite the bead your thread exited at the start of step 2 [d–e].

tip Stitch the same number of scallops at the top and bottom of the bracelet to create a neat closure; this bracelet has 13.

5 Repeat steps 3 and 4, but at the end of step 4, sew through the side Berry bead along the opposite edge [fig. 2]. Continue in this manner until you reach the desired length, keeping in mind that the bracelet will shrink a bit when adding the peyote edging. Don't end the working thread or tail.

6 Add 2 yd. (1.8m) of Fireline to the beginning of the bracelet, exiting the first 11º added in step 2 [fig. 3, point a]. Work a peyote stitch by picking up an 11º, skipping the next 11º, and sewing through the following 11º [a–b]. Work another stitch with an 11º [b–c], and then sew through the next Berry bead and following 11º [c–d]. Work three peyote stitches using 11ºs, and then sew through the next Berry bead and the following 11º [d–e].

● Berry bead
● 11º seed bead

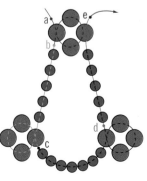

fig. 1

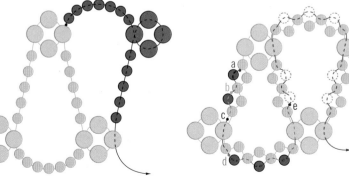

fig. 2

fig. 3

7 Continue following the existing thread path from the chevron base, adding two peyote stitches in the center of the bracelet and three peyote stitches along the edges. Check the fit, and add or remove chevron units as needed.

8 Using one of the tails, exit a center 11º on one end of the bracelet, and continue through the next 11º. Pick up five 11ºs, and sew through the 11º before the 11º your thread exited at the start of this stitch to form a ring [fig. 4]. Retrace the thread path, and end the tail. Repeat on the other end, and then end any remaining threads.

9 Open a jump ring, and attach half of the clasp to the seed bead ring on one end of the bracelet. Repeat on the other end.

Purple and blue bracelet

For this version, use more seed beads between the Berry beads to create a more open weave. I used cylinder beads in this bracelet (seven beads down the middle of the bracelet and nine beads along the edges). I also used 11º seed beads along the edges to bring in more color.

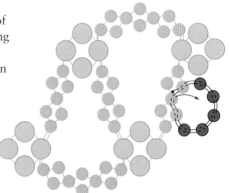

fig. 4

---

design option earrings

COLORS

7x4mm Swarovski pendant
   (Art. #6007, crystal)
Berry beads: Miyuki 2440,
   transparent gray rainbow luster
11º seed beads: Toho PF565,
   metallic sage

To make a pair of earrings, stitch a ring of Berry beads as in step 1, and then pick up 19 11º seed beads. Sew through the opposite Berry bead in the ring, and pick up seven 11ºs. Sew through the first Berry bead and the first 11º of the loop of 19. Work two peyote stitches using 11ºs, five stitches using Berry beads, and two stitches using 11ºs. Retrace the thread path of the loop of seven 11ºs, add a crystal drop, and end the thread.

Cottage Garden

This design reminds me of a fairy-tale cottage trellis with lovely little flowers and vines creeping up the sides. Right-angle weave provides a symmetrical structure, while peanut beads add dimension and soft connections.

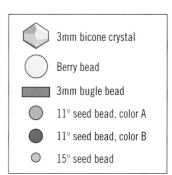

SUPPLIES

Pink and green bracelet,
7¼ in. (18.4cm)
- 44 3mm bicone crystals
- 3 grams Berry beads
- 5–6 grams 3mm bugle beads
- 11º seed beads:
   2–3 grams color A
   1 gram color B
- 4 grams 15º seed beads
- 4 4–6mm jump rings
- 2-strand clasp

Gold and green bracelet,
7 in. (18cm)
- 4–5 grams peanut beads
- 6–7 grams 3mm bugle beads
- 11º seed beads:
   2–3 grams color A
   1–2 grams color B
   (or 1 gram 15ºs)
- 6 4–6mm jump rings
- 3-strand clasp

For both bracelets:
- Fireline, 6-lb. test
- Beading needles, #12
- 2 pairs of chainnose pliers

COLORS

Pink and green bracelet

3mm bicone crystals: Swarovski, olivine
Berry beads: Miyuki 4201, Duracoat galvanized silver
3mm bugle beads: Miyuki 2441, cinnamon gold luster
11º seed beads: Toho 359, pale blue-lined light topaz (color A); Toho 313SFS, semi-matte cranberry (color B)
15º seed beads: Toho 457, gold-lustered green tea

Gold and green bracelet

Peanut beads: 1652, galvanized gold
3mm bugle beads: Miyuki 462, metallic gold iris
11º seed beads: Toho 323, gold-lustered olivine
15ºs seed beads: Toho 457, gold-lustered green tea

First row

1 On 2 yd. (1.8m) of Fireline, pick up four Berry beads, leaving a 10-in. (25cm) tail. Sew through the first Berry bead again to form a ring [fig. 1, a–b].

2 Pick up a color-B 11º seed bead, and sew through the opposite Berry bead in the ring, sew back through the B, and sew through the Berry bead your thread exited at the start of this step [b–c].

3 Pick up a color-A 11º seed bead, and sew through the next Berry bead in the ring. Repeat three times [c–d]. Sew through the next five beads in the flower unit [fig. 2, a–b].

4 Pick up a pattern of a 15º, a 3mm bugle bead, a 15º, and an A three times [b–c], and then pick up a 15º, a 3mm bugle, and a 15º. Sew through the A your thread exited at the start of this stitch to form a ring [c–d]. Retrace the thread path, skipping the As to pull the bugle bead unit into a diamond shape, and then exit an A opposite the A your thread exited at the start of this stitch [d–e].

5 Pick up a pattern of a Berry bead and an A three times, and then pick up a Berry bead. Sew through the A your thread exited at the start of this step, and the next Berry bead [fig. 3, a–b]. Pick up a B, and sew through the opposite Berry bead in the ring, back through the B just picked up, and through the Berry bead your thread exited at the start of this stitch [b–c]. Retrace the thread path through the ring of As and Berry beads, skipping the As. Sew through outer ring to exit the A opposite the connecting A in the bugle unit [c–d].

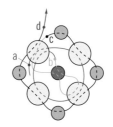

fig. 1

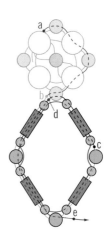

fig. 2

fig. 3

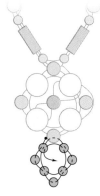

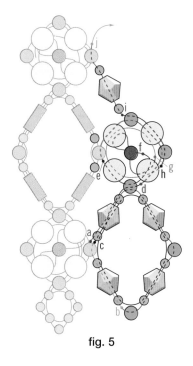

fig. 4

fig. 5

6 Repeat steps 4 and 5 until you reach the desired length, ending with step 5.

7 Pick up seven 15ºs and sew through the end A. Retrace the thread path, skipping the corner beads if desired to pull the beads into a diamond shape [fig. 4], and then end the thread. Repeat this step on the other end of the bracelet.

Second row

1 Add 2 yd. (1.8m) of thread to the end of the first row, exiting a side A [fig. 5, point a].

2 Pick up a pattern of a 15º, a 3mm bicone crystal, a 15º, and an A three times [a–b], and then pick up a 15º, a 3mm, and a 15º. Sew through the A your thread exited at the start of this step to form a ring [b–c]. Retrace the thread path, skipping the As to pull the crystal unit into a diamond shape, and then exit an A adjacent to the A your thread exited at the start of this stitch [c–d].

3 Pick up a pattern of a Berry bead and an A two times, and then pick up a Berry bead. Sew through the side A of the next bugle bead unit in the previous row [d–e]. Pick up a Berry bead, and sew through the A your thread exited at the start of this step and the next Berry bead in the ring [e–f]. Pick up a B, and sew through the opposite Berry bead in the ring, back through the B just picked up, and through the Berry bead your thread exited at the start of this stitch [f–g]. Retrace the thread path through the ring of As and Berry beads, skipping the As [g–h]. Sew through the outer ring to exit the A adjacent to the connecting A in the bugle bead unit [h–i]. Pick up a 15º, a 3mm, and a 15º, and sew through the side A in the next Berry unit [i–j].

4 Continue working in the established pattern, connecting the side As of each unit to the previous row, ending with a crystal unit.

Third row

Work the third row as in the first row, connecting the side As to the previous row.

Clasp

Open a jump ring and attach half of the clasp to a ring of 15ºs on one end of the bracelet. Repeat to attach the remaining rings.

Gold and green bracelet

Work as in the bugle bead and crystal bracelet, but omit the 3mm crystals, use all 3mm bugle beads, and substitute 15ºs in place of Bs.

design option
earrings

COLORS
3mm bicone crystals: Swarovski, olivine
Berry beads: Miyuki 4201, Duracoat galvanized silver
11º seed beads: Toho 359, pale blue-lined light topaz (color A); Toho 313SFS, semi-matte cranberry (color B)
15º seed beads: Toho 457, gold-lustered green tea

For a pair of earrings, make one Berry bead unit and one crystal unit. Make a ring of 15ºs as in step 7 opposite the crystal unit to attach an earring finding.

Herringbone Twist

Peanut beads and cube beads stitched in
herringbone are a lively combination. Insert
columns with a twist, and you'll create a band full of
texture and color!

SUPPLIES

Bracelet, 7½ in. (19.1cm)
- 6–7 grams peanut beads
- 2–3 grams 1.8mm cube beads
- 2–3 grams 15º seed beads
- Clasp
- 4 4–6mm jump rings
- Fireline 6-lb. test
- Beading needles, #12
- 2 pairs of chainnose pliers

COLORS

Peanut beads: F457B, matte
   metallic brown
1.8mm cube beads: Toho 183,
   hybrid opaque ultra luster gray
15º seed beads: Toho 307, hybrid
   turquoise Picasso

1 On 3 yd. (3.7m) of Fireline, pick up two cube beads, leaving a 10-in. (25cm) tail. Sew back through the cubes again, stacking them next to each other with the holes parallel [fig. 1, a–b]. Pick up a cube, and sew back through the previous cube and the new cube [b–c]. Repeat [c–d] for a ladder base of four cubes, then zigzag back through the base row [d–e].

2 Pick up two peanut beads, and sew through the next two cubes in the previous row [fig. 2, a–b]. Pick up two peanut beads, and sew through the next cube in the previous row. To turn at the end of the row, pick up a 15º seed bead, and sew back through the last peanut bead picked up [b–c].

3 Pick up two cube beads, and sew through the next peanut bead in the previous row. Pick up a 15º, and sew up through the next peanut bead in the previous row [c–d]. Pick up two cube beads, and sew through the next peanut bead in the previous row and the edge cube bead in the first row [d–e]. Pick up a 15º, and sew back through the edge peanut bead and the last cube bead picked up [e–f].

4 Repeat steps 2 and 3 twice, but in step 2, pick up a 15º between the two stitches as in step 3 [f–g].

5 Pick up 12 cube beads, skip the last two cubes, and sew back through the next 10 cubes. Sew through the next cube in the previous row [fig. 3, a–b]. Pick up a 15º, and sew up through the next cube in the previous row [b–c]. Pick up 12 cube beads, skip the last two cubes just picked up, and sew back through the next 10 cubes. Sew through the next cube in the previous row, the peanut bead below, and the cube below the peanut bead [c–d]. Sew back through the edge 15º, the peanut bead, and the edge cube [d–e].

peanut bead

1.8mm cube bead

15º seed bead

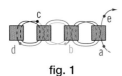

fig. 1

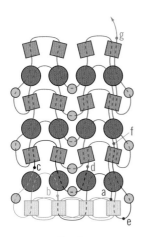

fig. 2

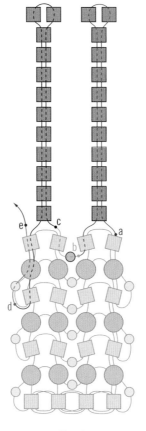

fig. 3

6 Pick up 22 15°s, wrap them around the first column twice, and sew through the first end cube at the top of the column [**fig. 4, a–b**]. Sew back through the adjacent cube and the next 10 cubes in the column, the following cube in the previous row, the 15°, and the next cube in the row [**b–c**]. Pick up 22 15°s, and embellish the column, wrapping around the column twice and sewing through the first end cube [**c–d**]. Sew back through the column, and turn at the end of the row by sewing through several existing beads. Sew through the column to exit the end cube at the top of the column [**d–e**].

tip **If necessary, twist the columns as you add the next row of peanut beads to keep the spiral of the 15°s uniform.**

7 Work steps 2 and 3 three times, picking up a 15° between the two stitches as before.

8 Work steps 5 and 6.

9 Repeat steps 7 and 8 three times, then work step 7. Zigzag through the last row of cubes to mimic the first row of cubes.

10 Exiting an edge cube on one end, pick up seven 15°s, and sew through the next two cubes in the previous row [**fig. 5, a–b**]. Pick up seven 15°s, and sew through the last cube in the row, the peanut bead below [**b–c**], and the cube below the peanut bead [**c–d**]. Sew back through the edge 15°, the peanut bead, and the edge cube [**d–e**]. Retrace the thread path of the 15°s, and end the thread. Repeat this step on the other end of the bracelet.

11 Open two jump rings, and attach one half of the clasp to both seed bead rings. Repeat on the other end.

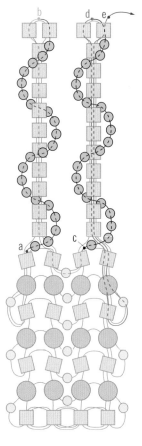

fig. 4

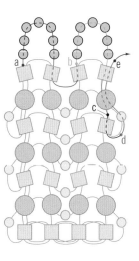

fig. 5

design options wide bracelet and earrings

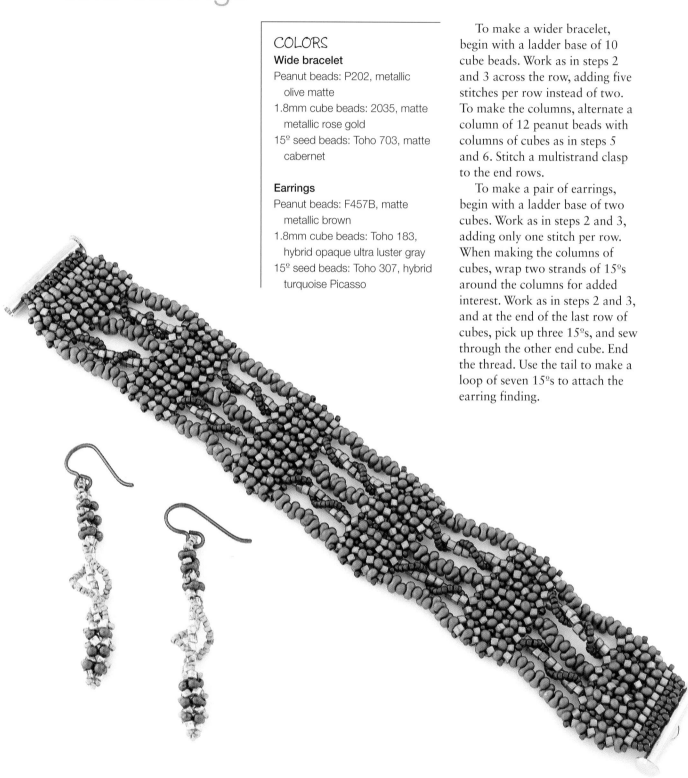

COLORS

Wide bracelet

Peanut beads: P202, metallic olive matte

1.8mm cube beads: 2035, matte metallic rose gold

15º seed beads: Toho 703, matte cabernet

Earrings

Peanut beads: F457B, matte metallic brown

1.8mm cube beads: Toho 183, hybrid opaque ultra luster gray

15º seed beads: Toho 307, hybrid turquoise Picasso

To make a wider bracelet, begin with a ladder base of 10 cube beads. Work as in steps 2 and 3 across the row, adding five stitches per row instead of two. To make the columns, alternate a column of 12 peanut beads with columns of cubes as in steps 5 and 6. Stitch a multistrand clasp to the end rows.

To make a pair of earrings, begin with a ladder base of two cubes. Work as in steps 2 and 3, adding only one stitch per row. When making the columns of cubes, wrap two strands of 15ºs around the columns for added interest. Work as in steps 2 and 3, and at the end of the last row of cubes, pick up three 15ºs, and sew through the other end cube. End the thread. Use the tail to make a loop of seven 15ºs to attach the earring finding.

Darling Drops

Use right-angle weave and netting to combine long drops and seed beads into beaded beads, and incorporate these cute components in earrings, bracelets, or necklaces. Since they use only a few beads each, they're a great way to use up beads in your stash.

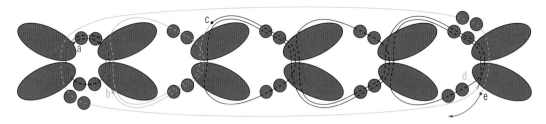

fig. 1

SUPPLIES

Beaded bead, ¾ x ½ in. (1.9x1.3cm)
- 12 long drops
- 1 gram 11º seed beads
- 1 gram 15º seed beads
- Fireline 6-lb. test
- Beading needles, #12

COLORS

Gold/green beaded bead (p. 45, upper left)

Long drops: Miyuki, gold iris
11º seed beads: Miyuki 359, pale blue-lined light topaz
15º seed beads: 15-9462, gold iris

Blue/purple beaded bead (upper right)

Long drops: Miyuki, metallic blue iris
11º seed beads: Toho 479, purple permanent galvanized
15º seed beads: Toho 505, higher metallic dragonfly

Gray/purple beaded bead (lower left)

Long drops: Miyuki, matte metallic dark gray
11º seed beads: Toho 89, metallic moss
15º seed beads: Toho, silver-lined violet

Purple beaded bead (lower right)

Long drops: Miyuki 460, metallic dark raspberry
11º seed beads: Toho 89, metallic moss
15º seed beads: Toho, silver-lined violet

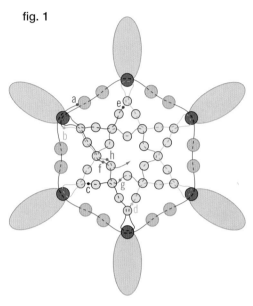

fig. 2

1 On 1 yd. (.9m) of Fireline, pick up two 11º seed beads, a long drop (with the bead's point facing away from the tip of the needle), a long drop (with the bead's point facing the tip of the needle), two 11ºs, a long drop (with the bead's point facing away from the tip of the needle), and a long drop (with the bead's point facing the tip of the needle), leaving a 6-in. (15cm) tail. Sew through the first two 11ºs and the next two long drops picked up in this step **[fig. 1, a–b]**.

2 Pick up two 11ºs, a long drop (with the bead's point facing away from the tip of the needle), a long drop (with the bead's point facing the tip of the needle), and two 11ºs. Sew through the two long drops your thread exited at the start of this stitch, and continue through the first four beads picked up in this stitch **[b–c]**. Repeat this step three more times **[c–d]**.

3 Pick up two 11ºs, and sew through the two end long drops from the first stitch. Pick up two 11ºs, and sew through the two end long drops from the last stitch **[d–e]**. Retrace the thread path to secure the join, and then sew through the next two 11ºs.

4 Pick up an 11º, and sew through the next pair of 11ºs on the same side. Repeat this step to complete the round, and step up through the first 11º picked up in this step **[fig. 2, a–b]**.

5 Pick up five 15º seed beads, skip the next two 11ºs, sew through the following 11º, and sew back through the last 15º picked up in this step **[b–c]**.

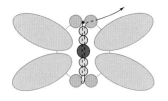

fig. 3

⬭ long drop	
⬤ 11º seed bead	
○ 15º seed bead	

6 Pick up four 15ºs, skip the next two 11ºs, sew through the following 11º, and sew back through the last 15º picked up in this step [c–d]. Repeat this step three more times [d–e].

7 Pick up three 15ºs, sew down through the first 15º picked up in step 5, sew through the adjacent 11º, sew back through the 15º above the 11º you just sewed through, and continue through the next two 15ºs, exiting the center 15º in the first stitch added in step 5 [e–f].

8 Pick up a 15º, skip the next three 15ºs in the previous round, and sew through the following 15º [f–g]. Repeat this step to complete the round [g–h], and then sew through the 15ºs added in this round to form a tight circle. Sew through the beadwork to exit the first 11º in a pair of 11ºs picked up in steps 2 and 3.

9 Pick up two 15ºs, an 11º, and two 15ºs. Sew under the thread between the corresponding 11ºs on the opposite side of the beaded bead, and sew back through all the beads picked up in this step [fig. 3]. Sew through the next three beads to exit the first 11º in the next pair of 11ºs on this side of the beaded bead. Repeat this step five more times, and then sew through the beadwork to exit a pair of 11ºs on the other side of the beaded bead.

10 Repeat steps 4–8 on this side of the beaded bead, and end the working thread and tail.

· ·

design option more beads

Use other drops, daggers, and lentil-shaped beads to make other sizes and shapes of beaded beads.

COLORS

Large dagger beaded bead

5x16mm dagger beads: Czech DAG-72, brushed bronze and copper peacock

11º seed beads: Toho 581, gilt-lined rust opal

15º seed beads: Toho 464A, deep silver

Silver/copper beaded bead

Lentil beads: Czech, silver with copper polka dots

11º seed beads: Toho 581, gilt-lined rust opal

15º seed beads: Toho 711, nickel

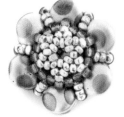

Ring-a-ling

An easy way to display your favorite drops or daggers is to stitch a peyote band and make loops that hold your beads front and center. Spaced with seed beads, these loops nestle together nicely.

SUPPLIES

Ring
- 24 6mm lentil drop beads
- 1 gram 1.5mm cube beads
- 2 grams 11º cylinder beads
- 1 gram 15º seed beads
- Fireline 6-lb. test
- Beading needles, #12

COLORS

6mm lentil drop beads: Czech, assorted matte colors

1.5mm cube beads: Toho 90, amethyst gunmetal

11º cylinder beads: Miyuki 1010, metallic earth batik luster

15º seed beads: Toho 39, silver-lined tanzanite

Ring band

1 On 2 yd. (1.8m) of Fireline, pick up six 11º cylinder beads, leaving a 6-in. (15cm) tail. Skip the last two cylinders, and sew back through the following cylinder, working toward the tail **[fig. 1, a–b]**. Work one peyote stitch using a cylinder, and then work a modified odd-count turn: Pick up a cylinder, and sew back through the first cylinder added in this step, working away from the tail **[b–c]**.

2 Work two stitches using cylinders **[fig. 2]**.

3 Work two stitches using cylinders. Work an odd-count turn: Pick up a cylinder, sew under the thread bridge between the last two edge cylinders, and sew back through the last cylinder picked up **[fig. 3]**.

4 Repeat steps 2 and 3 until you have eight cylinders along each edge of the band. End after completing step 3 **[fig. 4, a–b]**.

5 Work as in steps 2 and 3, but use 1.5mm cube beads until you have six cubes along each edge, and end after completing step 2 **[b–c]**.

6 Repeat steps 2 and 3 using cylinders until the band fits around your finger, ending after completing step 2 **[c–d]**.

7 Zip up the end rows **[fig. 5]**. Retrace the thread path, and end the threads.

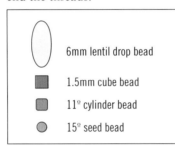

- 6mm lentil drop bead
- 1.5mm cube bead
- 11º cylinder bead
- 15º seed bead

Loop

1 Add 1 yd. (.9m) of Fireline, exiting a cube in the first row of cube beads added. Make sure your thread is exiting the cube bead pointing toward the adjacent edge row **[fig. 6, point a]**.

2 Pick up a pattern of a 15º seed bead and a lentil drop three times, and then pick up a 15º. Sew through the other cube bead in the same row, in the same direction **[a–b]**. Sew through the next two cubes in the ring band, exiting the cube bead your thread exited at the start of this step. Retrace the thread path through the loop and the cubes in the band, but exit the cube bead adjacent to the one your thread exited at the start of this step **[b–c]**.

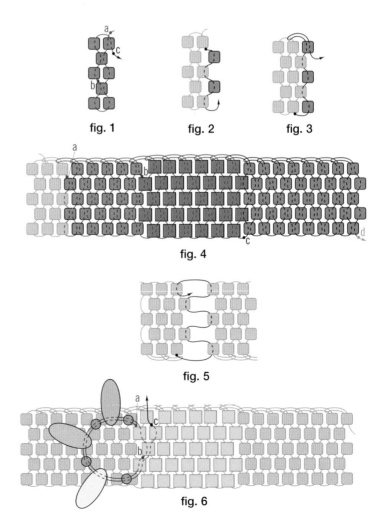

fig. 1   fig. 2   fig. 3

fig. 4

fig. 5

fig. 6

3 Pick up a repeating pattern of a lentil drop and a 15º three times, and then pick up a lentil drop. Sew through the other cube bead in the same row, in the same direction. Sew through the next two cubes in the ring band, exiting the cube bead your thread exited at the start of this step. Retrace the thread path through the loop and the cubes in the band, but exit the cube bead adjacent to the one your thread exited at the start of this step.

4 Repeat steps 2 and 3 until you have seven loops. Exit an edge bead.

Edge embellishment

1 Pick up two 15ºs, lay them along the edge of the band, and sew through two corresponding beads along the edge. Sew through the two 15ºs again. Repeat this step [fig. 7] along the edge of the band, snugging the 15ºs together as you go.

2 Sew through all the 15ºs on this edge. Don't pull too tight, or you might snug the beads too much, making the band too small to fit your finger.

3 Sew through the beadwork to exit the other edge of the band, and repeat steps 1 and 2. End the thread.

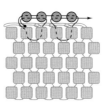

fig. 7

design option rings

COLORS

Green ring

4x6mm fringe drops: Czech, opaque turquoise Picasso

10º cylinder beads in place of 1.5mm cube beads: Miyuki 0380, matte metallic khaki iris

11º cylinder beads: Miyuki 371, matte metallic olive gold

Purple ring

3mm fringe drops: Magatamas, purple mix

1.5mm cube beads: Toho 90, amethyst gunmetal

11º cylinder beads: Toho 502, higher metallic plum iris

You can easily use any type of drop for this design. I omitted the edge embellishment for a more casual version using 4x6mm fringe drops and 3mm drops. Of course, you can go the other way and glam this ring to the max by using crystal drops. Another option is to make a band of all 1.5mm cube beads or 10º cylinder beads long enough to make a bracelet, and make sections of seven loops, skipping three rows between sections.

Drop Dead Daggers

Incorporate a dose of danger into individual odd-count peyote stitch components, injecting fierce style into an otherwise subdued stitch. Layer these components on a contrasting peyote stitch base for a substantial bracelet, but soften the edges with delicate lacy netting.

SUPPLIES

Bracelet 6½ in. (16.5cm)
- 108 3x10mm dagger beads
- 10º cylinder beads:
  7 grams color A
  6 grams color B
- 2–3 grams 11º seed beads
- 2-strand tube clasp
- 4 6mm jump rings
- Fireline 6-lb. test
- Beading needles, #12
- 2 pairs of chainnose pliers

COLORS

Dagger beads: Czech, gold smoke
  topaz luster
10º cylinder beads: Miyuki 0380,
  matte metallic khaki iris (color A);
  Miyuki 0005, medium blue iris
  (color B)
11º seed beads: Miyuki 452,
  metallic dark blue iris

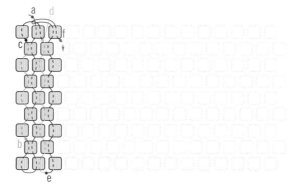

○ 3x10mm dagger bead
▢ 10º cylinder bead, color A
■ 10º cylinder bead, color B
○ 11º seed bead

fig. 1

Base

1 On a comfortable length of Fireline, pick up 10 color-A 10º cylinder beads, leaving a 6-in. (15cm) tail. Skip the last two As, and sew back through the next A toward the tail [fig. 1, a–b]. Work three peyote stitches using As [b–c]. Work a modified odd-count turn: Pick up an A, and sew back through the first A picked up in this step, working away from the tail [c–d].

2 Work four peyote stitches using As [d–e].

3 Work four peyote stitches using As. Work an odd-count turn: Pick up an A, sew under the thread bridge between the last two edge As, and then sew back through the A just picked up [e–f].

4 Repeat steps 2 and 3 until you reach the desired length, ending and adding thread as needed. Make sure both ends have a row of four As; then end the working thread and tail.

Small component

1 On 18 in. (46cm) of Fireline, pick up three color-B 10º cylinder beads, three 3x10mm dagger beads, and four Bs, leaving an 8-in. (20cm) tail. Skip the last two Bs, and sew back through the next B [fig. 2, a–b]. Work one peyote stitch with a B, sewing through the next dagger bead, one stitch with a dagger bead (positioning the four daggers to point the same direction), and one stitch with a B. Work a modified odd-count turn with a B [b–c].

2 Work four peyote stitches using Bs along this side of the component. Sew through the adjacent edge B [c–d], and then work four peyote stitches using Bs along this side of the component [d–e].

fig. 2

3 Work a decrease row: Sew through the adjacent edge B and the next B in the previous row [e–f]. Work three peyote stitches using Bs, and then sew through the next B [f–g]. Repeat this step on the other side of the component [g–h].

4 Don't end the working thread or tail; these will be used to attach the small components to the base. Make a total of six small components.

Large component

1 On 24 in. (61cm) of Fireline, pick up four Bs, one dagger, and five Bs, leaving a 10-in. (25cm) tail. Skip the last two Bs, and sew back through the next B **[fig. 3, a–b]**. Work three stitches using Bs, and then work a modified odd-count turn with a B **[b–c]**.

2 Work one stitch with a B, two stitches using daggers, and one stitch with a B **[c–d]**.

3 Work one stitch with a B and three stitches using daggers, and then work an odd-count turn with a B **[d–e]**.

4 Work four stitches using daggers **[e–f]**.

5 Stitch the next five rows as a mirror image of the first half of the large component, working odd-count turns along the edge with the tail **[f–g]**.

6 Work four stitches using Bs. Work a decrease turn: Sew under the thread bridge between the two adjacent edge Bs, and then sew back through the next two Bs on this side, exiting the last B added **[fig. 4, a–b]**.

7 Work three stitches using Bs. Work a modified decrease turn: Sew under the thread between the next two Bs in the previous two rows, and then back through the next two Bs on this side, exiting the last B added **[b–c]**.

8 Work two stitches using Bs, and then work a modified decrease turn **[c–d]**.

9 Work one stitch with a B **[d–e]**.

10 Using the tail, sew through the adjacent B, working toward the other side of the

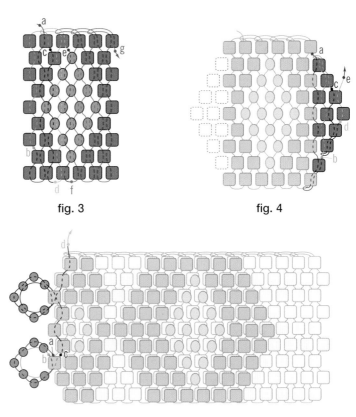

fig. 3

fig. 4

fig. 5

component. Repeat steps 6–9 on this side of the component.

11 Don't end the working thread or tail. Make a total of five large components.

Assembly

1 Position a small component on one end of the base. Align the two Bs on the edge with the tails between the first three edge As of the base. Stitch the small component in place by sewing through an edge A in the base, and then sew back through the B. Working along this side of the small component, stitch the Bs to corresponding As in the base, and then end the thread. Repeat with the remaining thread on the other side of the small component.

2 Position a large component next to the small component so the B in the last row of the large component and the center B in the last row of the small component will share the same

A in the base. Stitch the large component to the base in the same manner as the small component.

3 Alternating small and large components, stitch the remaining components to the base.

Embellishment

1 Add 2 yd. (1.8m) of Fireline to a small component on one end of the bracelet, exiting an outer B in the last row **[fig. 5, point a]**.

2 Pick up seven 11º seed beads, and sew through the B your thread just exited **[a–b]**. Retrace the thread path through the 11ºs, skipping every other 11º to pull the beads into a diamond shape, exiting the B **[b–c]**.

3 Sew through the next four Bs, and then repeat step 2. Sew through the next two Bs **[c–d]**.

fig. 6

4 Sew through the beadwork to exit the first edge A in the base on this end of the bracelet [fig. 6, point a]. Pick up five 11ºs, skip an A along the edge, and sew through the next two edge As and back through the last 11º added [a–b].

5 Pick up six 11ºs, skip an A along the edge, and sew through the next two edge As and back through the last 11º added [b–c].

6 Pick up four 11ºs and sew through the next two edge As and back through the last 11º added [c–d]. Repeat this step once [d–e].

7 Pick up six 11ºs, skip an A along the edge, and sew through the next two edge As and back through the last 11º added [e–f].

8 Pick up four 11ºs and sew through the next two edge As and back through the last 11º added [f–g].

9 Repeat steps 5–8 along this edge.

10 Sew through the beadwork to exit the first B in the end row, and then repeat steps 2 and 3 on this end of the bracelet.

11 Repeat steps 4–9 along the remaining edge of the bracelet, and end the thread.

12 Open four 6mm jump rings, and attach the loops of the clasp to the rings of 11ºs on the ends of the bracelet.

COLORS

Green ring

4x15mm daggers: Czech, olivine luster

10º cylinder beads: Miyuki 0003, dark green metallic iris

11º seed beads: Toho 457, gold lustered green tea

Black ring

3x10mm daggers: Czech, jet and black diamond

10º cylinder beads: Miyuki 254, bronze luster

11º seed beads: Miyuki 4221, Duracoat galvanized light smoky pewter

design option rings

Use the large component as a focal point for a funky ring. At the center of 2 yd. (1.8m) of Fireline, work a large component, and use the remaining tails to work an odd-count ring band five beads wide. Work the desired number of rows off of each side of the large component, and then zip up the end rows. Make an edge embellishment: Exiting an edge bead, pick up three 11ºs, and sew through the next two edge beads. Repeat this stitch along both edges. Sew through the beadwork to exit the first edge bead of the large component. Pick up three 11ºs, sew through the next two edge beads, and sew back through the last 11º added. Pick up four 11ºs, sew through the next two edge beads, and sew back through the last 11º added. Pick up two 11ºs, sew through the next two edge beads, and sew back through the last 11º added. Repeat this embellishment along the other edge of the large component.

Petal Pendant

Daggers and drops are perfect for petals. The wide range of shapes and colors will have you making a garden full of flowers. Add a loop to hang them as pretty pendants, or string a few strands on the back to make a bold ring.

SUPPLIES

Pendant, 1½ in. (3.8cm)

- 14 7x12mm curved drops
- 7 3x10mm dagger beads
- 7 3mm fringe drops
- 7 3mm bicone crystals
- 1 gram 11º seed beads
- 1 gram 15º seed beads
- 8mm jump ring
- Chain or necklace cord
- Fireline 6-lb. test
- Beading needles, #12
- 2 pair of chainnose pliers

COLORS

7x12mm curved drops: black

3x10mm dagger beads: Czech, brown iris

3mm fringe drops: Magatamas, purple iris

3mm bicone crystals: Swarovski, metallic light gold

11º seed beads: Toho 278, gold-lined topaz

15º seed beads Toho 459, gold-lustered dark topaz

1 Center a needle on 2 yd. (1.8m) of Fireline. Working with doubled thread, pick up 14 15º seed beads, and tie the beads into a ring with a square knot, leaving a 6-in. (15cm) tail. Sew through the first 15º again **[fig. 1, a–b]**.

2 Pick up two 15ºs, an 11º seed bead, and two 15ºs. Skip the next 15º in the ring, and sew through the following 15º **[b–c]**. Repeat to complete the round, and step up through the first three beads added in this round **[c–d]**.

3 Pick up a 3mm bicone crystal, and sew through the 11º in the next stitch of the previous round **[d–e]**. Repeat this step to complete the round **[e–f]**.

4 Flip your beadwork so the crystals are on the bottom of the ring. Pick up a 15º, a 3mm drop bead, and a 15º, and sew through the next 11º between the two 3mm crystals in the previous round **[fig. 2, a–b]**, positioning the 3mm drop bead on top of the next 3mm crystal in the previous round. Repeat this step to complete the round, and step up through the first 15º and 3mm drop bead added in this round **[b–c]**.

5 Pick up a 15º, a 3x10mm dagger, and a 15º, and sew through the next 3mm drop bead in the previous round **[c–d]**. Repeat this step to complete the round, and step up through the 15º, dagger, and 15º of the first stitch added in this round **[d–e]**.

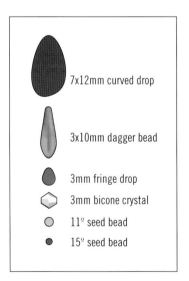

7x12mm curved drop

3x10mm dagger bead

3mm fringe drop

3mm bicone crystal

11º seed bead

15º seed bead

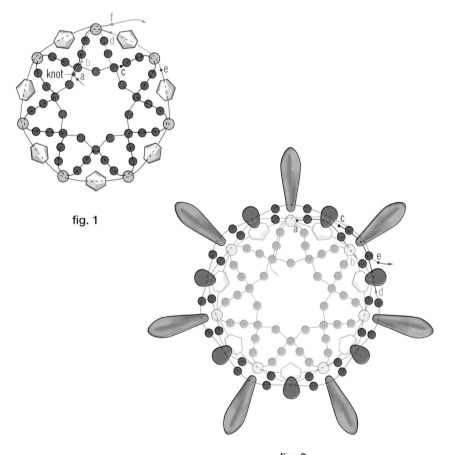

fig. 1

fig. 2

56

6 Pick up a 15º, a 7x12mm large curved drop, and a 15º, and sew through the next 15º, dagger, and 15º in the previous round **[fig. 3, a–b]**. Repeat this step to complete the round, and step up through the first 15º, 7x12mm drop, and 15º added in this round **[b–c]**.

7 Pick up an 11º, and sew through the next 15º, 7x12mm drop, and 15º added in the previous round **[c–d]**. Repeat this step to complete the round, and step up through the first 11º added in this round **[d–e]**.

8 Pick up two 15ºs, an 11º, and two 15ºs, and sew through the next 11º in the previous round **[fig. 4, a–b]**. Repeat to complete the round, and step up through the first three beads added in this round **[b–c]**.

9 Pick up a 15º, a 7x12mm drop, and a 15º, and sew through the 11º in the next stitch of the previous round **[c–d]**. Repeat this step to complete the round, exiting an 11º **[d–e]**.

10 Pick up nine 15ºs, and sew through the 11º your thread exited at the start of this step **[fig 5, a–b]**. Sew through the next 15º, 7x12mm drop, and 15º in the previous round, and the following 11º **[b–c]**.

11 Pick up two 15ºs, an 11º, and two 15ºs. Skip the next 15º, 7x12mm drop, and 15º, and sew through the following 11º **[c–d]**. Repeat this step to complete the round, and then step up through the first three beads added in this round **[d–e]**.

12 Pick up an 11º, and sew through the center 11º in the next stitch of the previous round **[e–f]**. Repeat this step to complete the round, and step up through the first 11º added in this round **[f–g]**. End the working thread and tail.

13 Open an 8mm jump ring, and attach it to the ring of 15ºs and a chain or necklace cord.

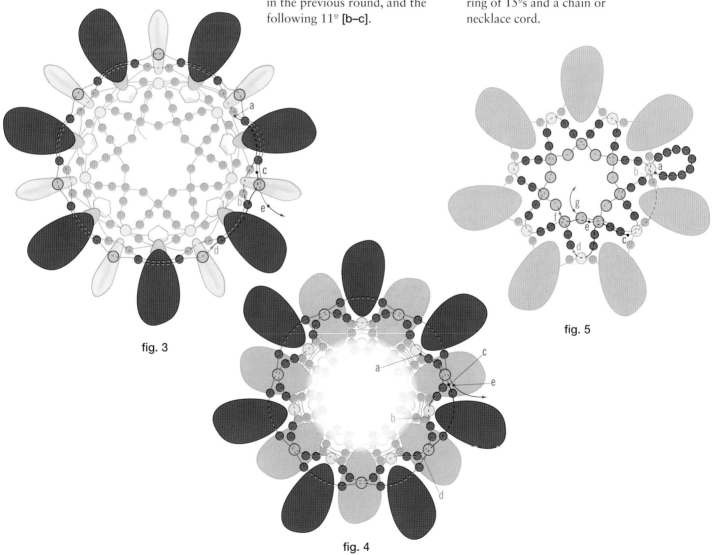

fig. 3

fig. 4

fig. 5

design option pendant and ring

COLORS

Green pendant

5x16mm dagger beads in place of the first round of 7x12mm curved drops: Czech, transparent blue luster

5x16mm dagger beads in place of the second round of 7x12mm curved drops: Czech, transparent green luster

3x10mm dagger beads: Czech, green iris

3mm drops: Magatama, amethyst-lined topaz

3mm bicone crystals: Swarovski, olivine

11º seed beads: Toho 512F, nickel-plated sage

15º seed beads: Miyuki 576, dyed smoky opaque silver-lined alabaster

Ring

7x12mm curved drops: black

5x16mm dagger beads in place of the first round of 7x12mm drops: Czech, matte opaque white with matte silver dots

3x10mm dagger beads: jet

3mm drops: Magatama, silver-lined crystal

3mm bicone crystals: Swarovski, white opal

11º seed beads: Toho 17282, silver-lined jet

15º seed beads: Miyuki 576, dyed smoky opaque silver-lined alabaster

Make a pendant using 5x16mm daggers in place of 7x12mm curved drops for an airy, spiky pendant. Or stitch a stunning floral motif ring by omitting the ring of 15ºs in step 10. Instead, complete the netted center as in steps 11 and 12, and exit an 11º in the inner ring of beads. Pick up enough 11º seed beads to wrap around your finger, and sew through an opposite 11º in the ring. Sew back through all the 11ºs just picked up, the 11º your thread exited on the first side of the ring, and the next 11º in the ring. Pick up enough 15ºs to equal the size of the band of 11ºs. Sew through an opposite 11º in the inner ring and back through all of the 15ºs just added. Sew through the 11ºs in the inner ring to exit an 11º adjacent to the other side of the band of 11ºs. Repeat for a second band of 11ºs.

58

Dagger & Pearl Pairing

Layer on the sparkle with rounds of crystals that support spikes of daggers. Link the dagger and crystal components with contrasting clusters of pearls in this gorgeous right-angle weave design.

- 6x12mm half-dagger
- 4mm crystal pearl
- 3mm bicone crystal
- 8º seed bead
- 15º seed bead

SUPPLIES

Bracelet, 7 in. (18cm)
- 24 6x12mm half-daggers
- 34 4mm crystal pearls
- 72 3mm bicone crystals
- 3 grams 8º seed beads
- 4 grams 15º seed beads
- Clasp
- 2 6mm jump rings
- Fireline 6-lb. test
- Beading needles, #12
- 2 pairs of chainnose pliers

COLORS

6x12mm half-daggers: Czech, moss

4mm crystal pearls: Swarovski, copper

3mm bicone crystals: Swarovski, olivine

8º seed beads: Toho 457, gold-lustered green tea

15º seed beads: Miyuki 1882, dark topaz gold luster

tip **Half-daggers have a flat edge and a rounded edge. I refer to the rounded edge as the top and the flat edge as the bottom. If you are using other types of daggers, it doesn't matter which way you pick them up.**

Dagger component

1 On 1 yd. (.9m) of Fireline, pick up three 15º seed beads, a 6x12mm half-dagger from bottom to top, a 15º, a 3mm bicone crystal, a 15º, and a dagger from top to bottom, leaving a 12-in. (30cm) tail. Sew through all the beads again to form a ring, exiting the bottom of the last dagger added in this step **[fig. 1, a–b]**.

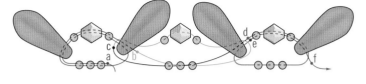

fig. 1

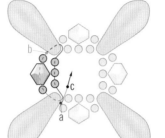

fig. 2

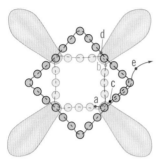

fig. 3

2 Pick up three 15ºs, a dagger from bottom to top, a 15º, a 3mm, and a 15º, and sew through the dagger your thread exited at the start of this step from top to bottom **[b–c]**. Sew through the first three 15ºs and the following dagger from top to bottom **[c–d]**.

3 Pick up a 15º, a 3mm, a 15º, a dagger from top to bottom, and three 15ºs, and sew through the dagger your thread exited at the start of this step from bottom to top **[d–e]**. Sew through the first 15º, 3mm, 15º, and the following dagger from top to bottom **[e–f]**.

4 Connect the first three stitches into a ring with a fourth stitch: Pick up three 15ºs, and sew through the unattached dagger from the first stitch from bottom to top **[fig. 2, a–b]**. Pick up a 15º, a 3mm, and a 15º, and sew through the dagger your thread exited at the start of this step from top to bottom **[b–c]**. Sew through the three 15ºs you just added and the following dagger from bottom to top. Zigzag through the stitches so there are equal thread paths through all of the beads.

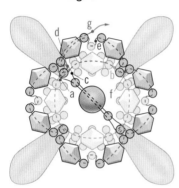

fig. 4

5 Using the tail, which should be exiting three 15ºs between two daggers, and working on the bottom of the component, pick up a 15º, and sew through the next three 15ºs **[fig. 3, a–b]**. Repeat three times, and then step up through the first 15º picked up in this step **[b–c]**. Pick up five 15ºs, skip three 15ºs, and sew through the next 15º added in the previous round **[c–d]**. Repeat three times, and then step up through the first three 15ºs added in this round **[d–e]**. End the tail.

6 Using the working thread and exiting a 15º, 3mm, and 15º, pick up a 15º, and sew through the next 15º, 3mm, and 15º **[fig. 4, a–b]**. Repeat three times, and then sew through the first 15º added in this step **[b–c]**.

7 Pick up a 15º, a 4mm pearl, and a 15º. Sew through the opposite 15º added in the previous step. Sew back through the 15º, 4mm, and 15º picked up in this step, and the 15º your thread exited at the start of this step [c–d].

8 Pick up a 15º, a 3mm, and a 15º, and sew through the center 15º in the next stitch of five 15ºs added in step 5 [d–e]. Pick up a 15º, a 3mm, and a 15º, and sew through the next 15º added in the previous round [e–f]. Repeat this step to complete the round, and step up through the first 15º, 3mm, and 15º added in this round [f–g]. Don't end the working thread.

9 Make a total of six dagger components.

End pearl cluster

1 On the component's bottom, with thread exiting a center 15º between two daggers, pick up a 15º, a 4mm, five 15ºs, a 4mm, three 15ºs, a 4mm, five 15ºs, a 4mm, and a 15º. Sew through the 15º your thread exited at the start of this step, and then sew through the first 15º and 4mm in the ring [fig. 5, a–b].

2 Pick up a 15º, an 8º seed bead, and a 15º, and sew

through the next 4mm and 15º [b–c]. Skip the next 15º in the ring, and sew through the following 15º and 4mm [c–d]. Repeat this step, and then sew through the first 15º, 8º, and 15º again [d–e].

3 Pick up a 15º, an 8º, and a 15º, and sew through the 15º, 8º, and 15º on the other side of the ring [e–f]. Repeat this step [f–g]. Sew through the beadwork to exit the outer ring, and retrace the thread path, skipping the center 15ºs to help define the shape. End the working thread.

4 Make a second end pearl cluster on another dagger component.

Pearl connector

1 Arrange a dagger component with an end pearl cluster so the dagger component thread is pointing toward the end, opposite the pearl cluster.

2 Pick up a 15º, a 4mm, five 15ºs, a 4mm, and a 15º, and sew through the corresponding 15º of the end component [fig. 6, a–b]. Pick up a 15º, a 4mm, five 15ºs, a 4mm, and a 15º, and sew through the 15º your thread exited at the start of this step. Sew through the first 15º and 4mm in the ring [b–c].

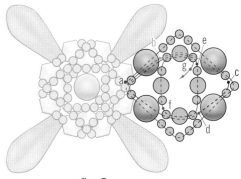

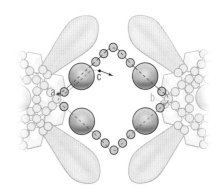

fig. 5

fig. 6

3 Repeat steps 2 and 3 of "End pearl cluster."

4 Connect the remaining dagger components.

5 Open a jump ring, and attach half of the clasp and an end pearl cluster on one end of the bracelet. Repeat on the other end.

design option ring

Pair a few of these units to make matching earrings, or nestle a dagger component between two pearl clusters for a fantastic focal point of a ring.

COLORS

3x10mm daggers: Czech, matte bronze

4mm crystal pearls: Swarovski, Tahitian-look

3mm bicone crystals: Swarovski, crystal golden shadow

8º seed beads: Toho 457, gold-lustered green tea

8º seed beads: Toho 998, gold-lined light jonquil AB

15º seed beads: Miyuki 456, gunmetal iris

Tiny Blossoms

Plant a scattering of flower blooms along an organic pathway of Herringbone stitch. Work a second layer of seed beads to fill in the holes while adding a splash of color and sparkle. The long drops create little flowers that look like springtime violets.

SUPPLIES

Bracelet, 7½ in. (19cm)

- 7–8 grams 3mm cube beads
- 80 4x7mm long magatamas
- 3 grams 11º cylinder beads
- 20 8º seed beads
- 4 6mm jump rings
- 2-strand tube clasp
- Fireline 6-lb. test
- Beading needles, #12
- 2 pairs of chainnose pliers

COLORS

3mm cube beads: Miyuki F463T, matte metallic green gold

Long magatamas: Miyuki 1527, sparkle celery-lined crystal

11º cylinder beads: Miyuki 1010, metallic earth batik luster

8º seed beads: Miyuki 2006, matte metallic dark bronze

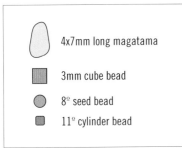

4x7mm long magatama

3mm cube bead

8º seed bead

11º cylinder bead

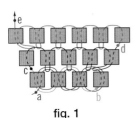

fig. 1

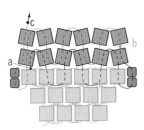

fig. 2

1 On 3 yd. (2.7m) of Fireline, pick up two 3mm cubes, leaving a 12-in. (30cm) tail. Sew back through the beads again, positioning them next to each other with holes parallel. Work in ladder stitch for a row of four cubes **[fig. 1, a–b]**. Zigzag back through the row so the working thread and tail are exiting opposite ends of the first bead **[b–c]**.

2 Work an increase row of brick stitch for a row of five cubes **[c–d]**. Repeat for a row of six cubes **[d–e]**.

3 Work a row of herringbone stitch: Pick up two cubes, and sew down through the next cube in the previous row and up through the following cube. Repeat to complete the row, exiting the last cube in the previous row. Pick up two 11º cylinder beads, and sew back through the last cube added **[fig. 2, a–b]**.

4 Work a row of herringbone stitch using cubes, but after picking up the two cubes for the last stitch in the row, sew down through the next two cubes in the previous two rows. Pick up two cylinders; sew back through the two cubes along the edge **[b–c]**.

5 Work a row of accelerated herringbone, picking up four beads instead of two: Pick up four long drops for the first stitch **[fig. 3, a–b]**, four cubes for the second stitch **[b–c]**, and four long drops for the third stitch. (Figures show back of the bracelet.) Pick up two cylinders; sew back through the last two edge beads **[c–d]**.

6 Work a row in regular herringbone stitch using two cubes per stitch, but for the last stitch in the row, sew down through three beads along the edge. Pick up two cylinders, and sew back through the last three edge beads **[d–e]**.

7 Work a row of accelerated herringbone: Pick up four cubes for the first stitch, four long drops for the second stitch, and four cubes for the third stitch. Pick up two cylinders, and sew back through the last two edge beads **[e–f]**.

8 Work a row in regular herringbone stitch using two cubes per stitch, but for the last stitch in the row, sew down through three beads along the edge, pick up two 11º cylinders, and sew back through the last three edge beads **[f–g]**.

9 Work a row of accelerated herringbone, picking up four beads instead of two: Pick up four long drops for the first stitch, four cubes for the second stitch, and four long drops for the third stitch. Sew down through the two beads along the edge, pick up two cylinders, and sew back through the last three edge beads.

10 Work a row in regular herringbone stitch using two cubes per stitch, but for the last stitch in the row, sew down through four beads along the edge. Pick up two cylinders, and

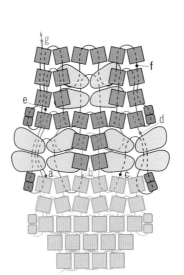

fig. 3

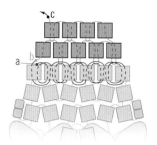

fig. 4

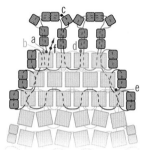

fig. 5

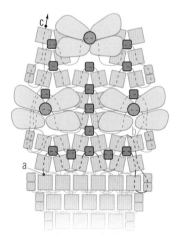

fig. 6

sew back through the last four edge beads.

11 Repeat rows 7–10 until you are within 1 in. (2.5cm) of the desired length, ending with step 9.

12 Work three rows of regular herringbone, using two cubes per stitch and cylinders to match the established turns.

13 Zigzag back through the last row of herringbone to mimic a ladder row [fig. 4, a–b]. Work two decrease rows of brick stitch (Basics) [b–c].

14 Exiting an end cube in the last row, pick up six cylinder beads. Sew down through the next cube in the row and back through the cube your thread exited at the start of this stitch [fig. 5, a–b]. Sew through the first two cylinders, pick up a cylinder, and sew through the next two cylinders [b–c]. Pick up a cylinder, sew through the next two cylinders, then sew through the next two cubes in the end row [c–d]. Repeat this step to make a second ring of cylinders.

15 Exiting the opposite end cube, pick up two cylinders, and sew through the end cube again and continue through the next cube along the edge [d–e]. Repeat to add a pair of cylinders to the end of each brick stitch row, sew through the beadwork to exit the other edge, and add a pair of cylinders to each end [e–f]. End the working thread.

16 Using the tail, repeat steps 13 and 14. End the tail.

17 Add 2 yd. (1.8m) of Fireline to the end you started on, exiting the end cube in the first row of herringbone. Pick up a cylinder, and sew through the next two cubes in the row. Repeat across the row, and then follow the established turn at the end of the row [fig. 6, a–b].

18 Continue adding cylinders between the obvious herringbone gaps, but omit them directly next to the long drops. As you work, add an 8º seed bead to the center of each flower motif: Sew through the first long drop, pick up an 8º, and sew through the fourth long drop. Repeat [b–c] for the length of the bracelet, and end the thread.

design option bracelet

For a quick and easy alternative, stitch up a bangle using accelerated herringbone, alternating four cubes with four long drops. Embellish the bangle with seed beads as desired.

COLORS
8º seed beads in place of 3mm cubes: purple-lined transparent olive AB

Long magatamas: Miyuki 2144, sparkle pink-lined crystal

15º seed beads in place of 11º cylinders: Toho Y307, opaque turquoise Picasso

Tulip Lace

Combine shapes using right-angle weave in this casual and comfortable bracelet. Tiny drops nestled delicately between long drops create a pretty edge embellishment.

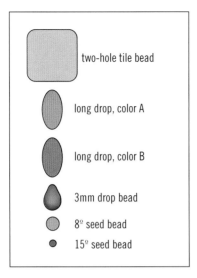

two-hole tile bead

long drop, color A

long drop, color B

3mm drop bead

8º seed bead

15º seed bead

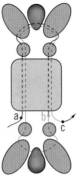

fig. 1

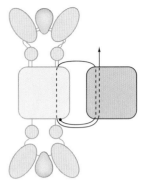

fig. 2

SUPPLIES

Bracelet, 7 in. (18cm)
- 27 two-hole tile beads
- 56 long drops, color A
- 52 long drops, color B
- 54 3mm drop beads
- 3–4 grams 8º seed beads
- Clasp
- 2 4–6mm jump rings
- Fireline 6-lb. test
- Beading needles, #12
- 2 pairs of chainnose pliers

COLORS

Bronze/green bracelet

Two-hole tile beads: Czech, metallic bronze

Long drops: Miyuki 2161, garnet-lined transparent light topaz AB (color A); Miyuki 457L, light bronze metallic (color B)

3mm drop beads: Miyuki, green iris

8º seed beads: Miyuki 457, dark bronze matte metallic

1 On a comfortable length of Fireline, attach a stop bead, leaving a 12-in. (30cm) tail.

2 Pick up a two-hole tile bead, an 8º seed bead, a color-A long drop (with the bead's point facing the tip of the needle), a 3mm drop bead, an A (with the bead's point facing away from the tip of the needle), and an 8º. Sew down through the second hole of the tile bead [fig. 1, a–b], and then pick up an 8º, an A (with the bead's point facing the tip of the needle), a 3mm, an A (with the bead's point facing away from the tip of the needle), and an 8º. Sew up through the first hole of the tile bead, continue through the next five beads, and sew through the second hole of the tile bead again [b–c].

3 Sew through the first hole of a new tile bead, the second hole of the previous tile bead, and the first hole of the new tile bead again [fig. 2].

4 Pick up a color-B long drop (with the bead's point facing away from the tip of the needle), an 8º, a 3mm, an 8º, and a B (with the bead's point facing the tip of the needle). Sew down through the second hole of the same tile bead [fig. 3, a–b]. Pick up a B (with the bead's point facing away from the tip of the needle), an 8º, a 3mm, an 8º, and a B (with the

bead's point facing the tip of the needle). Sew up through the first hole of the same tile bead, continue through the first five beads picked up in this step, and then sew down through the second hole of the same tile bead [b–c].

5 Repeat steps 2–4, alternating As and Bs, until you have used 27 tile beads or to the desired length, ending and adding thread as needed.

6 Pick up nine 15º seed beads, and sew through the second hole of the tile your thread exited at the start of this step [fig. 4, a–b]. Step up through the first 15º picked up, and then pick up a 15º, skip a 15º, and sew through the next 15º [b–c]. Repeat the last stitch three more times [c–d], and then sew through the second hole of the last tile bead again [d–e]. Retrace the thread path through the first nine 15ºs picked up in this step, and end the working thread. Remove the stop bead, and repeat this step using the tail on the other end of the bracelet.

7 Attach the clasp to the seed bead loops using jump rings.

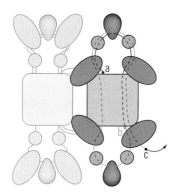

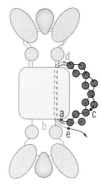

fig. 3   fig. 4

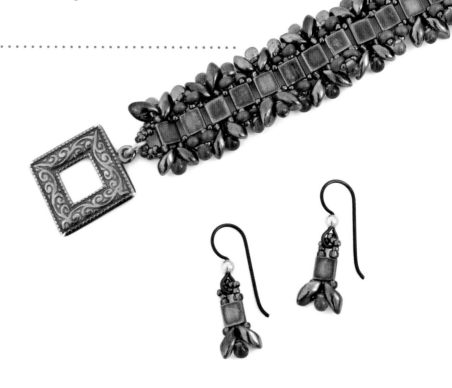

COLORS

Bracelet

Tila beads: Miyuki TL455, metallic variegated blue iris

Long drops: Miyuki LMA455, black metallic iris (color A)

3mm drops (in place of long drops): Miyuki F463B, green teal matte metallic iris (color B)

3mm drop beads: Miyuki 58L, Montana purple-lined, and Miyuki 57L, Montana sky-lined

11º seed beads: Miyuki 1426, silver-lined dark purple

15º seed beads: Toho 506, higher metallic June bug

Earrings

Tila beads: Miyuki TL455, metallic variegated blue iris

Long drops: Miyuki LMA455, black metallic iris (color A)

3mm drop beads: Miyuki 58L, Montana purple-lined (color B)

11º seed beads: Miyuki 1426, silver-lined dark purple

15º seed beads: Toho 506, higher metallic dragonfly

Design options Tila bead earrings and bracelet

Use Tila beads in place of two-hole tiles: You'll have to pick up a 15º seed bead before and after you pick up each new Tila bead in step 3. Also, I used smaller drops and seed beads when alternating between colors for the edge embellishment.

Make an adorable pair of earrings by picking up a single Tila bead or tile and then working the embellishment as in step 2 on one end. Work a simple loop on the other by picking up an 11º, seven 15ºs, and an 11º. Retrace the thread path through the beads, and end the threads. Attach an earring finding to the loop. Make a second earring.

Chunky Bangle

Weave a spiraling trail of Tila beads, peanut beads, crystals, and seed beads to create a wide yet wearable rope for a bangle loaded with texture.

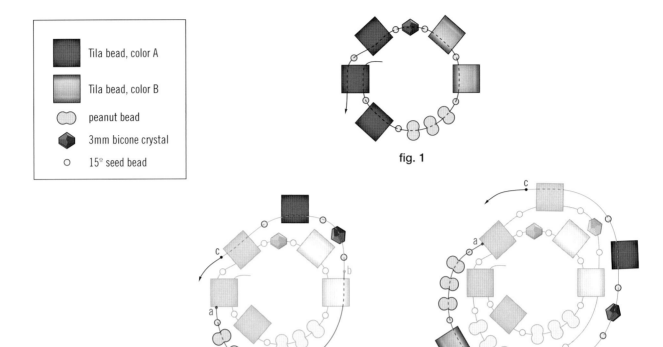

fig. 1

fig. 2

fig. 3

SUPPLIES

Bangle, 7¼ in. (18.4cm) inner circumference

- 72 Tila beads in each of 2 colors
- 216 peanut beads
- 72 3mm bicone crystals
- 4–5 grams 15º seed beads
- Fireline 6-lb. test
- Beading needles, #12

COLORS

Black/silver bangle

Tila beads: Miyuki TL401, matte black (color A); Miyuki TL1865, opaque smoke gray luster (color B)

Peanut beads: platinum

3mm bicone crystals: Swarovski, garnet satin

15º seed beads: Toho 711, nickel plated

1 On a comfortable length of doubled Fireline, attach a stop bead, leaving a 6-in. (15cm) tail. Pick up a color-A Tila bead, a 15º, an A, a 15º, three peanut beads, a 15º, a color-B Tila bead, a 15º, a B, a 15º, a 3mm bicone crystal, a 15º, an A, and a 15º. Sew through the remaining hole of the first A picked up in this step **[fig. 1]**. Flip the second A and B up toward the tail. If they get in the way while you stitch, thread the tail through the remaining holes of both beads to keep them out of the way.

2 Pick up a 15º, three peanut beads, a 15º, a B, and a 15º. Skip the next seven beads in the previous round, and sew through the remaining hole of the next B in the previous round **[fig. 2, a–b]**.

Pick up a 15º, a 3mm, a 15º, an A, and a 15º. Skip the next five beads in the previous round, and sew through the remaining hole of the next A in the previous round **[b–c]**.

3 Pick up a 15º, three peanut beads, a 15º, a B, and a 15º. Skip the next seven beads in the previous round, and sew through the remaining hole of the next B in the previous round **[fig. 3, a–b]**.

4 Pick up a 15º, a 3mm, a 15º, an A, and a 15º. Skip the next five beads in the previous round, and sew through the remaining hole of the next A in the previous round **[b–c]**.

5 Repeat steps 3 and 4 until you reach the desired length, ending and adding thread as needed, and stopping after you complete step 3. The beaded rope should reach around the widest part of your hand so it will slip over your hand but not fall off when the ends are joined.

tip The beadwork has a little bit of stretch to it, but you don't want to force the bangle too much or the stitches may break. To make a bracelet with a clasp, see the design option.

6 Align the ends so the spiral pattern matches up. (If needed, temporarily tie the remaining holes of the As together to hold them in place as you stitch, and then remove the temporary thread after the rounds are joined.) Pick up a 15º, a 3mm, and a 15º, and sew through the remaining hole of the B in the first round (the B flipped up in step 1). Pick up a 15º, and sew through the remaining hole of the B in the last round (the last B picked up).

7 Pick up a 15º, three peanuts, and a 15º, and sew through the remaining hole of the A in the first round (the A flipped up in step 1). Pick up a 15º, and sew through the remaining hole of the A in the last round (the last A picked up). Sew through several rounds, and end the working thread. Remove the stop bead, sew through several rounds in the other direction, and end the tail.

Design option clasp bracelet

To make a bracelet with a clasp, repeat steps 3 and 4 until you reach the desired length (minus the length of the clasp), and exit an A. Pick up a 15º, a 3mm, and a 15º, and sew through the remaining hole of the B in the previous round. Pick up nine 15ºs, and sew back through the same hole of the B your thread just exited to make a seed bead loop. Pick up a 15º, three peanut beads, and a 15º, and sew through the remaining hole of the A in the previous round. Pick up nine 15ºs, and sew back through the same hole of the A your thread just exited to make another seed bead loop. Sew back through several rounds, and end the working thread. Remove the stop bead, repeat this step with the tail, and end the tail. Attach a clasp to the pairs of loops on each end with jump rings.

COLORS

Tila beads and Czech tiles: Miyuki TL401, matte black (color A), and Czech, brown iris (color B)
Peanut beads in place of 3mm bicone crystals: Czech 2002, metallic olive
15º seed beads: Toho 459, gold-lustered dark topaz

Dramatic Daggers

This easy mulitstrand necklace showcases a favorite color or finish of large dagger beads nestled between peanut beads and offset with smaller daggers. Each strand is separated by Tilas or two-hole tile beads stitched into smart spacer bars.

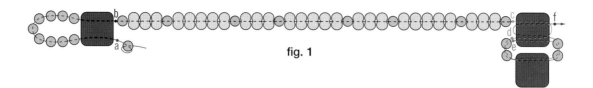

fig. 1

SUPPLIES
- 12 two-hole tile beads
- 453 peanut beads
- 19 5x16mm dagger beads
- 25 3x10mm dagger beads
- 2–3 grams 11º seed beads
- Clasp
- 2 4–6mm jump rings
- Fireline 6-lb. test
- Beading needles, #12
- 2 pairs of chainnose pliers

COLORS

Black/silver necklace, 16½ in. (41.9cm)

Two-hole tile beads: Czech, black

Peanut beads: Czech, silver-lined

5x16mm dagger beads: Czech, matte gray/black

3x10mm dagger beads: Czech, black

11º seed beads: Toho 614, matte brown iris

Purple necklace, 19½ in. (49.5cm)

Two-hole tile beads: Miyuki TL455, metallic variegated blue iris

Peanut beads: Miyuki BB2240, transparent gray rainbow luster

5x16mm dagger beads: Z69-94105, deep purple metallic glow

3x10mm dagger beads: Czech, black

11º seed beads: 39, silver-lined dark purple

tip If you use Berry beads, you may have to adjust the number of repeats in each section because they are a bit larger than peanut or farfalle beads. If you use Tila beads in place of two-hole tile beads, you may want make the center spacer bars with four Tilas instead of three because Tila beads are a little bigger than two-hole tiles.

1 On 2 yd. (1.8m) of Fireline, attach a stop bead, leaving a 6-in. (15cm) tail. Pick up a two-hole tile bead and nine 11º seed beads, and sew through the remaining hole of the tile bead [fig. 1, a–b]. Pick up a repeating pattern of an 11º, three peanuts, an 11º, and five peanuts three times, and then pick up an 11º, three peanuts, and an 11º [b–c].

2 To make a spacer bar: Pick up a tile bead, and sew through the other hole of the same tile just picked up [c–d]. Pick up two 11ºs, a tile bead, and two 11ºs. Sew through the second hole of the first tile bead picked up in this step [d–e]. Retrace the thread path through the last five beads just picked up and the second hole of the first tile bead, and then exit the top hole of the first tile picked up in this step [e–f].

3 Pick up a pattern of an 11º, three peanuts, an 11º, and five peanuts four times, and then pick up an 11º, three peanuts, and an 11º. Work as in step 2 to make a spacer bar with three tiles instead of two, and sew through the beads in the spacer bar to exit the top hole of the first tile picked up in this step.

4 Pick up a repeating pattern of an 11º, five peanuts, an 11º, and three peanuts seven times, and then pick up an 11º, five peanuts, and an 11º. Work as in step 2 to make a spacer bar with three tiles instead of two, and sew through the beads in the spacer bar to exit the top hole of the first tile picked up in this step.

5 Pick up 11ºs, peanuts, and tiles to make the second side of the necklace in a mirror image of the first, ending with a tile bead and nine 11ºs. Sew through the remaining hole of the last tile bead picked up.

6 Pick up a pattern of an 11º, five peanuts, an 11º, three peanuts, and an 11º three times, and then pick up an 11º, five peanuts, and an 11º. Sew through the bottom hole of the second tile bead in the next spacer bar.

7 Pick up a pattern of an 11º, five peanuts, an 11º, and three peanuts five times, and then pick up an 11º, five peanuts, and an 11º. Sew through the bottom hole of the third tile bead in the next spacer bar.

8 Sew through the tiles in the same spacer bar to exit the second hole of the first tile bead, making sure your thread is pointing toward the other end of the necklace.

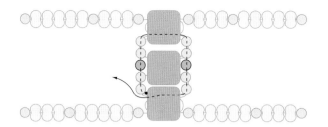

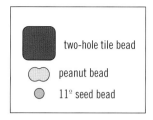

two-hole tile bead

peanut bead

11º seed bead

fig. 2

9 Pick up a pattern of an 11º, a peanut, an 11º, and a small dagger three times, and then pick up an 11º, a peanut, an 11º, and a large dagger. Alternate an 11º, a peanut, an 11º, and small and large daggers until you have seven large daggers, and then end with three small dagers. Sew through the second hole of the first tile bead in the next spacer bar. Sew through the tile beads in the same spacer bar to exit the bottom hole of the third tile bead, pointing toward the unfinished side of the necklace.

10 Pick up 11ºs and peanuts as in steps 7 and 6 to make the second strand on this side of the

necklace in a mirror image of the first side, exiting the remaining hole of the end tile bead.

11 Sew through the nine end 11ºs and the top hole of the end tile bead. End the working thread, remove the stop bead, and end the tail.

12 Add 1 yd. (.9m) of Fireline, leaving a 15-in. (38cm) tail and exiting the top hole of the third tile bead in one of the center spacer bars. Pick up a pattern of an 11º, three peanuts, an 11º, and five peanuts eight times, and then pick up an 11º, three peanuts, and an 11º. Sew through the

corresponding hole in the third tile bead of the other center spacer bar.

13 Sew through the bottom hole of the same tile bead, and pick up a pattern of an 11º, a peanut, an 11º, a small dagger, an 11º, a peanut, an 11º, and a large dagger until you have a total of 13 small daggers and 12 large daggers.

14 If desired, use the remaining threads to fill in 11ºs between the 11ºs along the edges of the spacer bars [fig. 2]. End the working thread and tail.

design option earrings

A loop of peanut beads and dagger beads makes a playful pair of earrings. On 1 yd. (.9m) of Fireline, pick up a two-hole tile bead and nine 11º seed beads, leaving a 6-in. tail. Sew through the remaining hole of the tile bead, and make a loop by picking up an 11º, 10 peanut beads, an 11º, a small dagger, a pattern of an 11º and a large dagger three times, an 11º, a small dagger, an 11º, 10 peanut beads, and an 11º. Sew through the first hole of the tile bead, the nine 11ºs above the tile, and the other hole of the tile bead. Sew through the beads in the loop, tie the working thread and tail together with a square knot, and end the thread. Attach an earring finding to the loop of nine seed beads. Make a second earring.

COLORS
Two-hole tile beads: Czech, metallic bronze
Peanut beads: Czech, silky gold iris
5x16mm dagger beads: Czech, brushed bronze and copper peacock
3x10mm dagger beads: Czech, transparent purple
11º seed beads: Toho 479, purple permanent galvanized

Checkered Cuffs

Work rounds of modified netting to create this everyday accessory. Dress it up by combining lots of shiny seed beads with crystals or make it understated by skipping the crystals and using matte-finish beads.

SUPPLIES

Bangle, 9 in. (23cm) inner circumference

- 48 two-hole tile beads
- 32 magatama long drops
- 48 Berry beads
- 16 4x7mm crystal pendants
- 2–3 grams 11º seed beads
- 2–3 grams 15º seed beads
- Fireline 6-lb. test
- Beading needles, #12

COLORS

Purple bangle

Two-hole tile beads: Czech, purple iris

Magatama long drops: Miyuki 455, black metallic iris

Berry beads: Miyuki 2441, cinnamon gold luster

4x7mm crystal pendants: Swarovski, light rose

11º seed beads: Toho 999M, gray-lined crystal AB

15º seed beads: Toho 711, nickel-plated silver

Green bangle

Two-hole tile beads: Czech, jet Picasso

Magatama long drops: Miyuki 460E, lichen matte metallic iris

Berry beads: Miyuki 263, sea foam-lined crystal rainbow

4x7mm crystal pendants: Swarovski, crystal AB

11º cylinder beads: Miyuki 1454, opaque alabaster light spring green

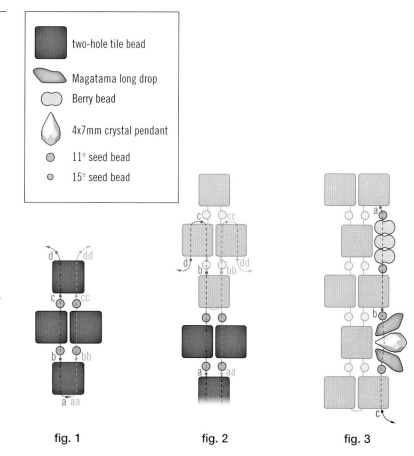

| two-hole tile bead |
| Magatama long drop |
| Berry bead |
| 4x7mm crystal pendant |
| 11º seed bead |
| 15º seed bead |

fig. 1   fig. 2   fig. 3

1 Thread a needle on each end of 4 yd. (3.7m) of Fireline. With one needle, sew through one hole of a two-hole tile bead, and with the other needle, sew through the remaining hole of the same tile bead [fig. 1, a–b and aa–bb].

2 With each needle, pick up an 11º seed bead, a tile bead, and an 11º [b–c and bb–cc]. With one needle sew through one hole of a tile bead, and with the other needle, sew through the remaining hole of the same tile bead [c–d and cc–dd]. Repeat this step 14 more times.

3 To join: With each needle, pick up an 11º, a tile bead, and an 11º. With each needle, sew through the corresponding hole of the first tile picked up in step 1 [fig. 2, a–b and aa–bb], the next 11º, and the following hole of the next tile bead [b–c and bb–cc]. With each needle, sew through the

remaining hole of the tile each thread is exiting [c–d and cc–dd].

💡 My bangle has 32 tile beads (counting 16 tiles on each edge), and measures 9 in. (23cm). Make sure the strand of beads is long enough to fit comfortably around the widest part of your hand. Adjust the length as needed, but the number of tile beads must be divisible by four so the edge embellishment can alternate evenly between long drops and peanut beads. To make a smaller bangle, pick up a total of 28 tile beads (14 along each edge); for a larger bangle, pick up a total of 36 (18 along each edge).

4 With one needle, pick up an 11º, three peanut beads, and an 11º, and sew through the remaining hole of the next tile bead along the same edge [fig. 3, a–b]. Pick up an

75

11º, a long drop (with the bead's point facing away from the tip of the needle), a 4x7mm crystal drop, a long drop (with the bead's point facing the tip of the needle), and an 11º. Sew through the remaining hole of the next tile bead along the same edge **[b–c]**. Repeat this step seven more times to complete the round. Repeat this step along the other edge of the bangle using the other needle.

5 With one needle, sew through the other hole of the same tile bead your thread is exiting. Pick up seven 15º seed beads, and sew through the outer hole of the next tile bead along the same edge **[fig. 4, a–b]**. Pick up seven 15ºs, and sew through the inner hole of the next tile bead along the same edge **[b–c]**. Repeat the last two stitches to complete the round, and then sew through the other hole of the tile bead your thread is exiting **[c–d]**.

6 Pick up two 15ºs, and sew through the three center 15ºs

from the previous round **[d–e]**. Pick up two 15ºs, and sew through the other hole of the next tile bead along the same edge **[e–f]**. Repeat this step to complete the round.

7 With the other needle, repeat steps 5 and 6 along the other edge of the bangle.

8 With one needle, sew through the beadwork to exit one hole of a tile bead in the center of the bangle, and work as in step 5, picking up seven 15ºs between each tile.

9 With the other needle, sew through the beadwork to exit the other hole of a tile bead in the center of the bangle. Work as in step 6, but pick up three 15ºs instead of two, and only sew through one 15º instead of three.

10 With each needle, retrace the thread path back out to the edge rounds, and end the threads.

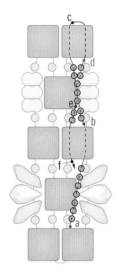

fig. 4

Design option slim bangle

Tila beads have a slimmer profile than two-hole tile beads, so if you like the look, use Tila beads to make a slender version of this bangle, and omit the crisscross seed bead embellishments.

COLORS

Tila beads: Miyuki 2008, green pink matte metallic iris

Magatama long drops: Miyuki 457L, light bronze metallic

Peanut beads: Japanese, metallic gunmetal green

11º seed beads: Toho 994, gold-lined rainbow crystal

Sparklers

Nestle a small rivoli in a netted bezel, and then suspend it from a right-angle weave floral motif. Stitch one, and you'll quickly see the great design potential of these components!

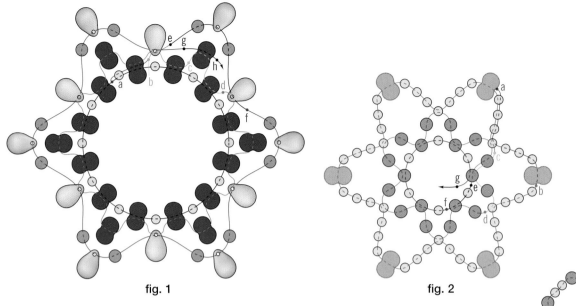

fig. 1

fig. 2

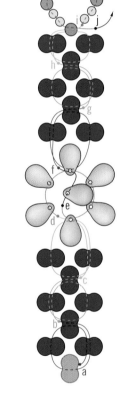

fig. 3

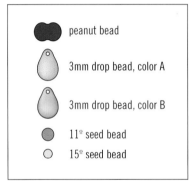	peanut bead
	3mm drop bead, color A
	3mm drop bead, color B
	11º seed bead
	15º seed bead

SUPPLIES
- 2 8mm rivolis
- 74 peanut beads
- 3mm drop beads:
    24 color A
    16 color B
- 1–2 grams 11º seed beads
- 1 gram 15º seed beads
- 2 earring findings
- Fireline 6-lb. test
- Beading needles, #12
- 2 pairs of chainnose pliers

COLORS
Rivolis: Swarovski, crystal vitrail
    medium
Peanut beads: metallic blue iris
3mm drop beads: Miyuki 58L,
    purple-lined Montana (color A);
    Miyuki 57L, sky-lined Montana
    (color B)
11º seed beads: Toho P479,
    permanent galvanized purple
15º seed beads: Toho 995,
    gold-lined aqua rainbow

1 On 1 yd. (.9m) of Fireline, pick up a pattern of a 15º seed bead and a peanut bead 12 times, leaving a 6-in. (15cm) tail. Tie the beads into a ring with a square knot, and exit a peanut bead **[fig. 1, a–b]**.

2 Pick up a color A 3mm drop bead, skip the next 15º in the ring, and sew through the next peanut bead **[b–c]**. Pick up a peanut bead, skip the next 15º in the ring, and sew through the next peanut bead **[c–d]**. Repeat this step to complete the round, and step up through the first A picked up in this round **[d–e]**.

3 Pick up an 11º seed bead, a color-B 3mm drop bead, and an 11º, and sew through the next A in the previous round **[e–f]**. Repeat this step to complete the

round **[f–g]**, and sew through the beadwork to exit a peanut bead picked up in step 2 **[g–h]**.

4 Pick up seven 15ºs, and sew through the next peanut bead in the same round **[fig. 2, a–b]**. Repeat this step to complete the round, and step up through the first four 15ºs picked up in this round **[b–c]**.

5 Pick up three 11ºs, and sew through the center 15º in the next stitch of the previous round [c–d]. Repeat this step to complete the round, and then step up through the first two 11ºs picked up in this round [d–e]. Insert an 8mm rivoli face down so the front of the rivoli rests on the beads in step 1.

6 Pick up a 15º, and sew through the center 11º in the next stitch of the previous round [e–f]. Repeat to complete the round [f–g], and then retrace the center ring, exiting a peanut bead from step 2.

7 Pick up three peanut beads, sew through the peanut bead your thread exited at the start of this step, and sew through the first two peanut beads picked up in this step [fig. 3, a–b]. Repeat this step [b–c].

8 Pick up a peanut bead, an A, and a peanut bead. Sew through the peanut bead your thread exited at the start of this step and the first two beads picked up in this step [c–d].

9 Pick up five As, and sew through the A your thread exited at the start of this step [d–e]. Pick up a 3mm, and sew through the opposite A in the ring [e–f].

10 Pick up three peanut beads, and sew through the A your thread exited at the start of this step and the first two peanut beads picked up in this step [f–g].

11 Pick up three peanut beads, and sew through the peanut bead your thread exited at the start of this step and the first two peanut beads picked up in this step [g–h].

12 Pick up a peanut bead, an 11º, and a peanut bead. Sew through the peanut bead your thread exited at the start of this step and the first two beads picked up in this step [h–i].

13 Pick up a pattern of two 15ºs and an 11º three times, and then pick up two 15ºs. Sew back through the 11º your thread exited at the start of this step [i–j], and then retrace the thread path, skipping the 11ºs to form a diamond shape. End the working thread and tail.

14 Open the loop of an earring finding, and attach the end loop created in step 13.

15 Make a second earring.

· ·

Design option ring

Use the main component to make a delightful ring, and embellish the outer edge with lots of sparkling crystals. To add crystal loops, exit a peanut bead picked up in step 2. Pick up a 15º, a color-C bicone crystal, 11 15ºs, a C, and a 15º. Sew through the peanut bead your thread just exited, and then sew through the beadwork to exit the next peanut bead from step 2. Make five more loops with 15ºs and Cs. Sew through the beadwork to exit the center 15º from the beads picked up in step 4. Pick up five 11ºs, and sew through the next loop of 15ºs and Cs from back to front. Pick up a color-D bicone crystal and five 11ºs. Sew through the previous loop of 15ºs and Cs from front to back, and then sew through the center 15º your thread just exited. Sew through the beadwork to exit the next center 15 from the beads picked up in step 4. Make five more loops using 11ºs and Ds, connecting the remaining loops of 15ºs and Cs. Use 11º and 15º seed beads to make a coordinating ring band in right-angle weave.

COLORS

Rivoli: Swarovski, crystal vitrail medium

Peanut beads: 2748, matte black rainbow

3mm drop beads: Miyuki 58L, purple-lined Montana (color A); Miyuki 57L, sky-lined Montana (color B)

4mm bicone crystals: Swarovski, light olivine (12 color C) and indicolite (6 color D)

11º seed beads: Toho P479, permanent galvanized purple

15º seed beads (Toho 995, gold-lined aqua rainbow)

Dainty Daisies

Suspend darling little daisies made with drop beads and peanut beads from the center of a feminine necklace.

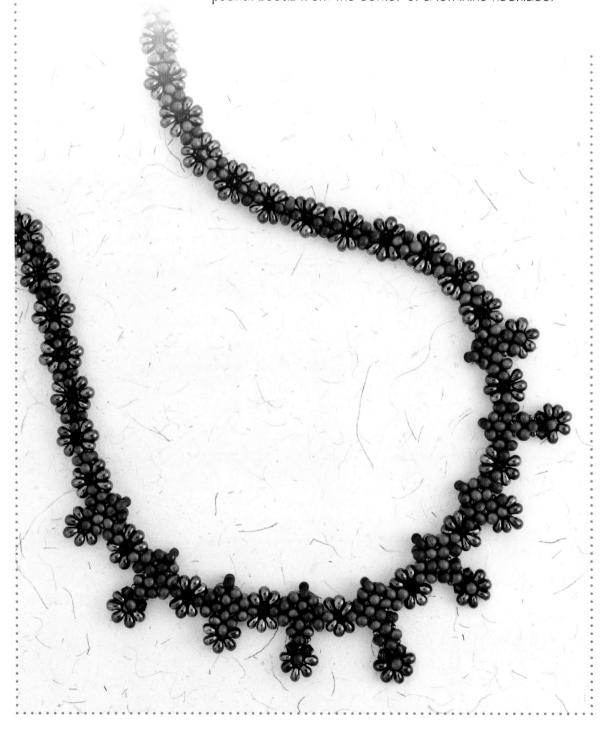

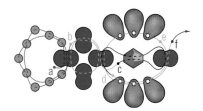

fig. 1

3mm drop bead

peanut bead

3mm bicone crystal

15º seed bead

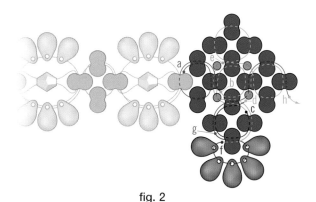

fig. 2

SUPPLIES

- 20–25 grams 3mm drop beads
- 25–30 grams peanut beads
- 42 3mm bicone crystals
- 3–4 grams 15º seed beads
- 2 6mm jump rings
- Fireline 6 lb. test
- Beading needles, #12
- Clasp
- 2 pairs of chainnose pliers

COLORS

3mm drop beads: Toho 505, higher metallic dragonfly

Peanut beads: F455c, multi blue iris matte

3mm bicone crystals: Swarovski, purple velvet

15º seed beads: Toho 5051a, higher metallic dragonfly

1 On 3 yd. (2.7m) of Fireline, pick up a peanut bead and nine 15º seed beads, leaving a 6-in. (15cm) tail. Sew through the peanut bead to form a ring, and then retrace the thread path, skipping the third, fifth, and seventh 15º to form a point [fig. 1, a–b], and exit the peanut bead. End the tail.

2 Pick up three peanut beads, and sew back through the peanut bead your thread exited at the start of this step. Sew through the first two peanut beads picked up in this step [b–c].

3 Pick up a 3mm bicone crystal and a peanut bead. Skip the peanut bead just picked up, and sew back through the crystal and peanut bead your thread exited at the start of this step in the same direction [c–d].

4 Pick up three 3mm drop beads, and sew through the peanut bead at the end of the crystal [d–e].

Pick up three drops, and sew through the peanut bead your thread exited at the start of this step. Sew through the first three drop beads picked up in this step and the next peanut bead [e–f].

5 Repeat steps 2–4 12 times.

6 Repeat step 2 [fig. 2, a–b].

7 Pick up three peanut beads, and sew through the peanut bead your thread exited at the start of this step.

8 Pick up a 15º, and sew through the next peanut bead in the previous stitch [b–c]. Pick up three peanut beads, and sew through the peanut bead your thread just exited [c–d]. Repeat this step two times [d–e], and then pick up a 15º and sew through the next peanut bead. Sew through the next four beads to exit the center peanut bead in the first stitch picked up in this step [e–f].

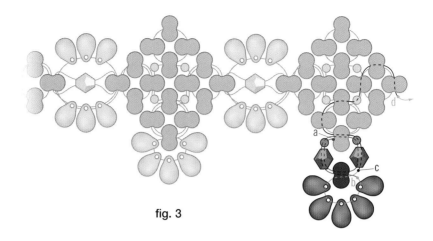

fig. 3

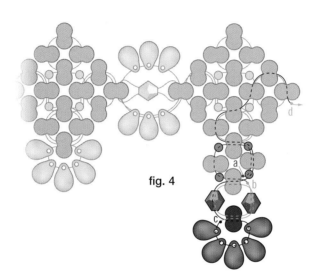

fig. 4

9 Pick up five drops and sew through the peanut bead your thread exited at the start of this step [f–g]. Sew through the beadwork to exit the center peanut bead in the stitch opposite the join of the last crystal unit [g–h].

10 Repeat steps 3 and 4, and then repeat steps 2, 7, and 8.

11 Pick up a 15º, a crystal, a peanut bead, a crystal, and a 15º. Sew back through the peanut bead your thread exited at the start of this step and the first 15º, crystal, and peanut bead picked up in this step [fig. 3, a–b]. Pick up five drop beads, and sew back through the peanut bead your thread exited

at the start of this stitch [b–c]. Sew through the beadwork to exit the center peanut bead in the stitch opposite the join of the last crystal unit [c–d].

12 Repeat steps 3 and 4, and then repeat steps 2, 7, 8, and 9.

13 Repeat steps 3 and 4, and then repeat steps 2, 7, 8, and 11.

14 Repeat steps 3 and 4, and then repeat steps 2, 7, 8, and step 2 again.

15 Pick up a 15º, and sew through the next peanut bead in the previous stitch. Repeat the last stitch three times [fig. 4, a–b].

Pick up a crystal, a peanut bead, and a crystal. Sew back through the peanut bead your thread exited at the start of this stitch, and the first crystal and peanut bead just picked up [b–c]. Repeat step 9 [c–d].

16 Work the second half of the necklace in a mirror image of the first half, ending and adding thread as needed.

17 Open a 6mm jump ring and attach the nine-bead loop and one half of the clasp. Repeat for the other end of the necklace.

Design option bracelet

To make a matching bracelet, work the center portion of the necklace, omitting the dangles. Alternate peanut bead colors within the diamonds to break up the solid shapes and add interest to the design.

COLORS

Drop beads: Toho F460G, steel green gold iris matte

Peanut beads: F459F, olive bronze metal matte (color A); F457N, burgundy bronze matte (color B)

3mm crystals: Swarovski, crystal silver shade

15º seed beads: Toho Y310, sour apple Picasso

BASICS REVIEW

THREAD & KNOTS

STOP BEAD ·

Use a stop bead to secure beads temporarily when you begin stitching. Choose a bead that is different from the beads in your project. Pick up the stop bead, leaving the desired length tail. Sew through the stop bead again in the same direction, making sure you don't split the thread. If desired, sew through it one more time for added security.

ADDING THREAD

To add a thread, sew into the beadwork several rows or rounds prior to the point where the last bead was added, leaving a short tail. Follow the thread path of the stitch, tying a few half-hitch knots between beads as you go, and exit where the last stitch ended. Trim the short tail.

ENDING THREAD

To end a thread, sew back through the last few rows or rounds of beadwork, following the thread path of the stitch and tying two or three half-hitch knots between beads as you go. Sew through a few beads after the last knot, and trim the thread.

HALF-HITCH KNOT ·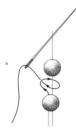

Pass the needle under the thread bridge between two beads, and pull gently until a loop forms. Cross back over the thread between the beads, sew through the loop, and pull gently to draw the knot into the beadwork.

SQUARE KNOT ·

1 Cross one end of the thread over and under the other end. Pull both ends to tighten the first half of the knot.

2 Cross the first end of the thread over and under the other end. Pull both ends to tighten the knot.

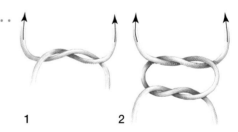

1   2

WIREWORK

OPENING AND CLOSING LOOPS AND JUMP RINGS · · · · · · · · · ·

1 Hold a loop or a jump ring with two pairs of chainnose pliers. (Flatnose or bentnose pliers can be used as well.)

2 To open the loop or jump ring, bring the tips of one pair of pliers toward you, and push the tips of the other pair away from you. Reverse the steps to close the open loop or jump ring.

1   2

STITCH BASICS

LADDER STITCH ·

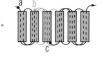

1 Pick up two beads, sew through the first bead again, and then sew through the second bead [a–b].

2 Add subsequent beads by picking up one bead, sewing through the previous bead, and then sewing through the new bead [b–c]. Continue for the desired length.

BRICK STITCH ·

1 Begin with a ladder of beads (see Ladder stitch), and position the thread to exit the top of the last bead. The ends of each new row will be offset slightly from the previous row. To work the typical method, which results in progressively decreasing rows, pick up two beads. Sew under the thread bridge between the second and third beads in the previous row from back to front. Sew up through the second bead added, down through the first bead, and back up through the second bead [fig. 1].

fig. 1

2 For the row's remaining stitches, pick up one bead per stitch. Sew under the next thread bridge in the previous row from back to front, and sew back up through the new bead. The last stitch in the row will be positioned above the last two beads in the row below, and the row will be one bead shorter than the previous row [fig. 2].

fig. 2

INCREASING WITH BRICK STITCH ·

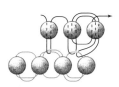

To increase at the beginning of the row, work as in brick stitch, but sew through the thread bridge between the first two beads instead of the second and third. To increase at the end of the row, add a second stitch to the final thread bridge in the row.

ZIPPING UP ENDS ·

To join two sections of a flat peyote piece invisibly, match up the two pieces so the edge beads fit together. "Zip up" the pieces by zigzagging through the up-beads on both edges.

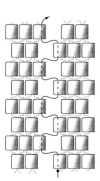

. . . .

PEYOTE: FLAT EVEN-COUNT

1 Pick up an even number of beads **[a–b]**. These beads will shift to form the first two rows.

2 To begin row 3, pick up a bead, skip the last bead strung in the previous step, and sew through the next bead in the opposite direction **[b–c]**. For each stitch, pick up a bead, skip a bead in the previous row, and sew through the next bead, exiting the first bead strung **[c–d]**. The beads added in this row are higher than the previous rows and are referred to as "up-beads."

3 For each stitch in subsequent rows, pick up a bead, and sew through the next up-bead in the previous row **[d–e]**. To count peyote stitch rows, count the total number of beads along both straight edges.

. . . .

PEYOTE: FLAT ODD-COUNT

Odd-count peyote is the same as even-count peyote, except for the turn on odd-numbered rows, where the last bead of the row can't be attached in the standard way because there is no up-bead to sew into. The odd-row turn can be convoluted, so I've simplified it here. Please note that the start of this simplified approach is a little different in that the first beads you pick up are the beads in rows 2 and 3. In the next step, you work row 1 and do a simplified turn. After the turn, you'll work the rest of the piece, beginning with row 4.

1 Pick up an odd number of beads **[fig. 1, a–b]**. These beads will shift to form rows 2 and 3 in the next step. If you're working a pattern with more than one bead color, make sure you pick up the beads for the correct rows.

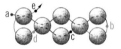

fig. 1

2 To begin the next row (row 3), pick up a bead, skip the last bead strung in the previous step, and sew through the next bead in the opposite direction **[b–c]**. Continue in this manner, exiting the second-to-last bead strung in the previous row **[c–d]**. For the final stitch in the row, pick up a bead, and sew through the first bead strung again **[d–e]**. The beads added in this row are higher than previous rows and are referred to as "up-beads."

3 To work row 4 and all subsequent even-numbered rows, pick up one bead per stitch, exiting the end up-bead in the previous row **[fig. 2, a–b]**.

fig. 2

4 To work row 5 and all subsequent odd-numbered rows, pick up one bead per stitch, exiting the end up-bead in the previous row **[b–c]**. Pick up a bead, and sew under the thread bridge between the edge beads below **[c–d]**. Sew back through the last bead added to begin the next row **[d–e]**.